M(other)land

'This is the kind of book I wish I had access to as a young mum' Nadiya Hussain

'A brilliant book not just on parenthood but on what makes us the people we are . . . everyone has something to gain by reading it' Poorna Bell

'Priya has written a thought-provoking memoir of being raised between cultures and how this has impacted her parenting of her daughter' Devi Sridhar, author of *Preventable*

'We can all learn something from this brilliant, must-read book' Julia Samuel, leading British psychotherapist and bestselling author

ABOUT THE AUTHOR

Priya Joi is a well-respected science journalist with a career spanning twenty years and has worked for organizations including the World Health Organization, the *Lancet* and *New Scientist*. She reported on the Ebola outbreak in West Africa and the COVID-19 pandemic, and has reported from the field on malaria, HIV and TB. She has freelanced for the *Guardian*, the BBC and Médecins Sans Frontières, and has chaired and spoken at science conferences. Joi has worked to shine a light on issues of race, sexism and discrimination her entire career. *M(other)land* is her first book.

T0182324

M(other)land

A Memoir on Race, Identity and Belonging

PRIYA JOI

PENGUIN LIFE

AN IMPRINT OF

PENGUIN BOOKS

PENGUIN LIFE

UK | USA | Canada | Ireland | Australia
India | New Zealand | South Africa

Penguin Life is part of the Penguin Random House group of companies
whose addresses can be found at global.penguinrandomhouse.com.

First published 2023
This edition published 2024
001

Typeset by Jouve (UK), Milton Keynes
Printed and bound in Great Britain by Clays Ltd, Elcograf S.p.A.

The authorized representative in the EEA is Penguin Random House Ireland,
Morrison Chambers, 32 Nassau Street, Dublin D02 YH68

A CIP catalogue record for this book is available from the British Library

ISBN: 978-0-241-57432-4

www.greenpenguin.co.uk

*For Mum and Leela, the one who came before
me and the one who came after me.*

Contents

Prologue

'Mama, Mama, Mama! Can I have that?' I glanced up in the middle of the French supermarket we were in, meandering through highways of Camembert and baguettes and Côtes du Rhône, to see what Leela was pointing at.

In among a carousel of film merchandising tat, the thing that caught her eye was a blonde 'Elsa braid' from the Disney film Frozen.

We'd moved to France when Leela was only eleven months old, to a village on the border with Switzerland that lay in the hinterland between the Alps and the Jura Mountains. For the most part my kid was surrounded by white people in all-weather jackets and ironed jeans.

What did Leela think about her skin colour, I wondered, that she wanted a blonde hair extension? Did she think she was white? Was it true that children had no idea that people came in different colours?

'I'm happy to buy that for you, but don't you think it might look a bit odd sandwiched on to your black hair?' I asked, amused.

'I wish I had blonde hair.' Leela let out a sigh.

'You mean you want to dye your hair blonde one day?' I replied.

It was then my caramel-coloured child told me how she really felt. A confession that made my entire being implode like a dying star running out of energy, collapsing in on itself.

She crinkled her nose, and then cautiously, somehow sensing the impact it might have, revealed this heart-stopping confession:

'I want to be peach. I don't think brown skin is . . .' She searched for the right word, before settling on, 'beautiful.'

This was my first inkling that my daughter was not entirely at peace with the way she looked. At first, I wasn't sure she really meant it – that perhaps she was trying out a thought like kids do, rolling it around in their minds like a marble to see where it lands.

Because it didn't fit the idea I had of her. Leela has always been a bold and confident kid, who strides through the world like she owns it. The embodiment of female empowerment. So, what's with this dissatisfaction with her skin? Her words played back to me, this time without the pause. 'I want to be peach.'

Holy hell.

Deep breath, *I thought,* don't panic.

'Leela, we come from one of the oldest civilizations in the world. We come from a land where billions pray to mighty warrior goddesses every day. They're all brown.'

'So people in India aren't peach?'

'There's lots of different shades of brown. There's light brown, dark brown, peachy brown, even. Your skin tone is just another colour in your crayon box.'

'Hmm,' she shrugged. 'I still want the Elsa braid.'

Maybe it was a bit much to expect a four-year-old to engage in a discourse over her ancestry in the middle of Carrefour.

I don't know if what I said was the right way to respond. But I felt weary to my bones to still be living in the kind of world that has drip-fed the notion of white superiority into my girl's subconscious.

Through predominantly white Disney princesses, to rarely using brown or Black characters in advertising, to Band-Aids that are putty-coloured. Over and over, the drumbeat to our lives is that

2

white is most desirable. Even when we try to resist this indoctrination, it seeps in.

'Mama?' Leela was looking up at me with giant brown eyes, holding up the blonde Elsa braid, tugging on my jacket pleadingly. 'Can we buy it then?' I was a million miles away. Leela was slapping the side of my thigh more urgently now.

How could my kid understand how the planets revolve around the sun and yet be unclear on where she fitted in? I had to find a way to make her proud of her heritage and be bold enough to strut into the world knowing who she is, not wishing she was born as something different.

I wanted her to feel comfortable in her own skin and, to do that, I needed to help her reconcile her race and skin colour with her identity as a half-Indian, half-Bangladeshi British kid growing up in France. I needed to counteract the societal messaging by injecting enough self-worth and belief in her so that she never thinks of herself as lacking in any shape, form or colour.

But to do that, I was going to have to start with myself.

1. You Can't Be What You Can't See

From the age of seven, I had one of those diaries that comes with pages designed to be filled in with your favourite things – colours, foods, hobbies, what you wanted to be when you grew up. My career ambitions yo-yoed wildly from being a model or flight attendant (which I referred to in the more 1980s lingo of 'air hostess') when I was seven, to being a plastic surgeon (reconstructive rather than cosmetic, I noted in my diary) or a laboratory researcher when I was fifteen.

Reading back through these pages decades later, I'm startled by the shift in my ambitions between early childhood and adolescence. It makes sense considering that by the time I hit puberty I was an asthmatic, thick-glasses-wearing science nerd. I was a *Seinfeld* fan who loved English literature as much as maths and physics. Not exactly the groundwork for a glamorous career that would involve slinking around fashion shoots in a silk spaghetti-strapped dress or trotting down the aisle of a 747.

Mum signed me up for an extracurricular group called 'Alternatives', back when we lived in Bangalore. It was run by a couple who'd been trained in creative and critical thinking, with a mind to encourage Indian teenagers – who go through a rigid educational system of rote learning – to think a little differently.

We had a crash course in everything from art (discussing provocative artists like Picasso) to music (dancing around to Bob Marley's 'Buffalo Soldier' in both political understanding and groove). I doubt Mum knew exactly what the course involved, but my parents have always been encouraging of me and my sister trying out anything we wanted to (between us, over the years, we did ballet, classical Indian dance, tennis, rock climbing, and piano and guitar lessons).

Looking back, my life in Bangalore was so much freer (I used to take rickshaws all over the city from the age of fourteen), and more progressive, with classes like 'Alternatives', than my subsequent life in England.

When I moved back to England at sixteen in the early 1990s, everyone in my school wore Doc Marten boots, long floaty skirts and messy hair as an homage to the reigning king of grunge, Kurt Cobain. In India, Nirvana hadn't quite taken off in the same way just yet so I rocked up in my Garfield T-shirts and a padded hairband which I would wear with a quiff that paid bizarre homage to Elvis. Needless to say, I stood out.

There's an old joke that South Asian children have the freedom to choose whatever career path they want . . . as long as it's a doctor, engineer or lawyer. I mean, there's nothing wrong with these as occupations. It makes sense that immigrants want their children to have jobs with security, ones that will always be needed regardless of the state of the economy. But for so many young Asians who get routed into these careers irrespective of whether they wanted to be an artist or a writer, it narrows the field acutely.

Even though my parents had never been this over-bearing with me and my sister, and generally encouraged us to follow our hearts, the reason I felt so unable to imagine anything beyond an academic career is clear when you look at the role models that teenage me had – or rather the abysmal lack of any sort of representation for Asian, Black or Latina girls. This list is everyone I could think of and, as you can see, it isn't South Asian-specific but includes anyone remotely resembling my skin tone – we couldn't be picky back in those days.

1. Jasmine from *Aladdin*

The turquoise-blue-clad princess of Agrabah was the first Disney princess of colour, in the 1992 animation. She was pretty badass. Running away from the palace and escaping her domineering father and conniving adviser Jafar, all in search of freedom. Jasmine was curvy and dusky-skinned enough to seem relatable but what with her being royalty, having a tiger as a pet and marrying the Prince of Persia and all, she wasn't exactly someone I could realistically aspire to be . . .

2. Aishwarya Rai, Miss World 1994

Aishwarya was as unattainable a role model as the animated character of Jasmine but this was one of the first times I can remember an Indian woman being talked about in the West as being a great beauty. She also wasn't stick thin, which made her seem more relatable.

3. Scary Spice/Mel B

One of the most blatant media perpetuations of the myth of Black women as 'scary', this nickname was devised by Peter Loraine, editor of the British magazine *Top of the Pops*, who said he 'laughed the most when we came up with "Scary"'. Mel B has said in interviews that the band were happy just to go with the nicknames and she wasn't offended by it, but it never seemed to sit right with me that she was called that just because . . . she was a bit loud and had an afro?

4. Naomi Campbell

Although she would later be known for tantrums – famously throwing her phone at her assistant in 2007 – in the early 1990s she was all over MTV for writhing around with Michael Jackson in the hip-thrust-tastic music video for 'In the Closet'. She was the only woman I saw, alongside Iman, who was both dark-skinned *and* considered incredibly beautiful.

5. Brandy (Moesha) and Tia and Tamera Mowry

For me and my sister, in watching R&B singer Brandy in *Moesha*, and *Sister Sister* with the Mowry twins, we found the first representation of normal-ish girls going through normal-ish problems. Closer to our reality than supermodels at least.

6. Gita from *EastEnders*

This is the only portrayal of a South Asian woman on British TV I can remember from the 1990s. Her character was extremely unalluring (no shade to Shobu Kapoor who played her) and flip-flopped between being either angry or depressed (though, to be fair, Gita's husband did bugger off after she gave birth to have an affair with her sister). Her legendary catchphrase was 'Sanjay!' as she was always screeching for her husband. Incidentally, one of the most shame-inducing, soul-curdling moments of my life was when a white warm-up comedian at a TV filming I went to while I was at university let the camera hover on my face and yelled 'SANJAY!' in his imitation of an Indian accent, complete with signature head-bobble. Clearly this unfunny piece of human garbage is the one who should have been ashamed, but as he'd done the equivalent of a school bully by pointing and jeering and making an entire audience of 400 people roar with laughter, it was my face that went flame-red with embarrassment.

7. Sarita Choudhury in Mira Nair's *Kama Sutra*

In polar opposition to Gita, who sucked all the sexual tension from the screen, Sarita Choudhury, who played the princess Tara, was the embodiment of sex on screen. The film was so incredibly seductive, it earnt an instant ban by the Indian Censor Board when it came out in 1996. But it was groundbreaking in its portrayal of female desire and how women of colour could be sexy; empowering rather than shameful.

~

So there you have it. A list of every brown woman I could have remotely looked at as a role model. Only none of them truly felt like me. In retrospect, I could have viewed the lack of representation as a form of freedom – when there is no one telling you how or what to be, maybe it opens up the possibility of becoming anything you want. But this is the perspective that I have now, in my mid-forties, tired of the decades of feeling that society wants to hem me in as a woman, as a woman of colour. Back then, as a young teenager, it was different. At that age, in terms of our sense of self, we're still only just a hair's breadth away from when we were fluffy little ducklings, for whom the world can seem scary and impossible to navigate. What we all need is someone showing us the way, reaching out and asking us to take their hand. And when you venture into any new area, when you don't see anyone around who looks like you, it's easy to assume it's not for you.

I had little in the way of cultural connection with Black American teenagers like Moesha, Tia and Tamara (or at least the way they were portrayed in the shows), with televisions in their bedrooms, wearing full-on make-up to school, huddling with friends on their beds with their shoes on. While the other girls in my sixth form rocked intense eyeshadows and goth lipsticks, I made do with occasionally 'borrowing' Mum's lipstick. One morning at school, my lips smeared in a tomato-red lipstick and lit up like a beacon, I came out of biology class and ran straight into my mum.

'What the hell is that on your face?' she yelled, offering zero explanation as to why she was in my school in the first place.

I didn't have much of a comeback as a) I'd nicked her lipstick and b) bright red lips wasn't really an appropriate classroom look. I swallowed the urge to truthfully reply 'Dior 999' and instead ran to the school bathroom, upset at this impingement on my freedom and embarrassed in front of my friends. No more make-up at school for me, then.

I looked on in no small envy at my white friends having such a plethora of women to identify with. Anyone in the cast of *Friends* (funny), Cher from *Clueless* (carefree), Buffy the Vampire Slayer (kickass), Jen or Joey from *Dawson's Creek* (relatable), anyone from *Sex and the City* (fashionable), and practically any woman from any Hollywood movie ever made.

It wasn't until I had graduated from university and was in my first job as an editor at *The Lancet* medical journal that I heard about women like Kalpana Chawla, the Indian-born American astronaut, and even then it was only news because of her fatal flight in 2003 when the NASA space shuttle *Columbia* exploded as it re-entered earth's atmosphere.

Chawla would have been someone the teenage me could have related to, in all my bespectacled, nerdy, giant curly-haired glory. I knew South Asian women made fine lawyers, doctors, journalists and politicians, but apart from Indira Gandhi, I couldn't name a single one I'd seen in the public eye.

There were Bollywood heroines, of course, but I was under no illusion that boys saw me through the same exotic lens as they beheld those brown-skinned women. To the white boys around me, I felt as attractive as a household pet.

I brooded over why this might be on the way to a party one night. It was 1994, and I was squeezed into a car with my friends, all of us smelling like patchouli, and 'Murder She Wrote', the reggae dance-hall anthem by Chaka Demus & Pliers, on the radio.

For kids who grew up in the English countryside, parties were always down tiny country roads in the middle of nowhere. Whoever had got their driving licence and could handle the wheel while mildly drunk would be nominated to ferry everyone else home. Seeing as I attracted mostly sensible people as friends, it was hardly Russian roulette. The worst that would happen is someone would throw up in the back seat, the air adrift with the sickly smell of Diamond White. But every now and then I'd hear a story of kids being in cars that got wrapped around lamp posts as navigating pitch-black country roads got the better of someone with too much Malibu and Coke in them.

Like all Indian girls with strict parents, going out with friends felt like day release. But whereas for them going out meant 'getting off' with someone – that slightly grim phrase for kissing a boy – I had little hope I'd be getting off with anyone. The idea that I was desperate for the attention of skinny, pimply white boys who could barely grow a moustache may make me want to gag now, but as a teenager, with my hormones firing their pubescent launch sequence, all I wanted was to be noticed.

We piled out of the car and into a town hall decorated with streamers. I looked around me and quietly accepted that my night would be spent dancing with my friends, no boys in my orbit.

It didn't help that my mother and father, like many loving South Asian parents, were (and still are) my ultimate hype people.

'You can be anything you want to be,' my father would announce, with the same assurance with which he might state that the earth is round.

'You have such a beautiful face,' my mother would say, 'with a gorgeous smile that can win over any boy,' before quickly adding, 'when you are old enough to be interested in boys, that is.'

For a brief while I'd glow in such compliments. But the minute I was around a teenage boy, I'd become convinced that they saw me more as a Quasimodo character. I doubted Mum and Dad's definition of beautiful was the same as that of these white boys.

Brown and Black friends of mine have similar stories. Not just of being measured up against the popular girls and found wanting – that comes as standard in all teenage lives – but of feeling like they were competing in a different league, where none of the people you wanted to play with were there. A feeling that if you differed from the thin, able-bodied white girl ideal of beauty, you weren't in the running at all.

It's hard to know whether this was because the boys were conditioned to be drawn to the Kate Moss variety, or whether we ourselves had been convinced we were not desirable. My guess is a bit of both. The insidiousness of white supremacy means that everyone, whatever colour they are, is programmed to view pale skin as the epitome of attractiveness. I know so many brown boys (my husband included) for whom the posters on their bedroom wall growing up were of white women like Kim Basinger and Cindy Crawford. Across Asia and Africa, meanwhile, girls were lightening their skin with dangerous chemicals in the belief that their dark skin branded them unattractive – and though the body positivity movement has made some stop, skin bleaching is still depressingly common. Feeling not simply uncomfortable in our skin, but relegated to Uglyville because of it, wasn't exactly the best vibe to attract someone.

~

Leela has a richer variety of role models. The marketing machine has cottoned on to the fact that representing children of colour on the screen means a whole new boatload of merchandise can be peddled. The publishing world has caught up too, with a greater diversity of children's books featuring more Black and brown protagonists than ever before.

What reassures me is how bold Leela is in her aspirations.

'I want to be a scientist and an artist,' she'll announce casually. 'Or a vet and a baker.'

'Bakers have to wake up at the crack of dawn,' I'll respond, offering this as the only obstacle to her ambitions there. She's a night owl, and even at the age of seven struggles to wake up at eight a.m. for school, so I am doubtful.

'Hmm,' she'll consider. 'Then I'll be a vet and a fashion designer. They don't have to wake up early, right?'

I remember how wide open the world seemed to me too at that age. Dreaming big is not a problem for little kids – thinking up magical scenarios is all they know. The trouble comes, of course, when they grow up to be teenagers and are suddenly expected to pinpoint their exact career path. This has got to be the most bonkers thing we do in society: asking someone who has been alive for less than two decades to decide what job will best suit them in many years to come.

My mission from Day One has been to allow Leela to dream as big and wide and fantastical as her head sees fit. The world isn't a big old scary place to her. A combination of my husband Shabby's freebies at the wedding magazine he used to run and my subsequent World Health Organization salary meant we have travelled extensively. Leela has been to well over a dozen countries (a massive privilege that I'm well aware risks me sounding like a posh twat saying 'Oh yah, travel is the best education, don't you know?', especially given there are so many who struggle to take their kids to the local soft-play centre). But compared with friends who might prioritize a big house or new car, travel has always taken top billing for me.

'Why don't you save your money for a rainy day?' Mum used to ask whenever I packed my bags for another trip.

'You may have noticed it rains every day in England,' I'd remind her.

Growing up with a foot on each continent, I know full well the East isn't all power cuts and arranged marriages any more than the West is about wealth and glamour, even if that's how it seems to those looking out from their corners of the world, and my mission is to pass on this understanding to Leela.

Showing her how people live outside of Western Europe gives her access to all the possible lives she could lead. When you grow up only understanding the lifestyle, power structures and cultural attitudes of the West, everything to the East of it inevitably seems alien, somehow other.

Not only do I want Leela to see how diverse the world is, but how varied her own options are. No matter how much you experience when you travel and how much you learn about the world, exploring the planet teaches you fundamental truths about yourself and what you are capable of. Seeing people live in different ways offers tantalizing possibilities of what you too could be. Especially when you're a person of colour living in a country where others who look like you are not very visible on the TV, or making music, or writing books, and are constrained to a few professions, visiting countries where

Black or brown folk are in the majority and are doing whatever they damn please can be exhilarating and mind-expanding. I want my daughter's dreams to know no bounds, with no limits on what or who she can be. The trick for any mother is to figure out when to guide, when to steer and when to sit back and let her find her own way.

2. Being Brit(ish) in India

At eight years old, while still doodling my dream career choices, I was leaving my parents and sister in England and flying to India with my aunt for the foreseeable future. (The first time I did that, I was a four-month-old baby, but that's a story I'll unravel later.) I don't recall being devastated, possibly because I wasn't fully aware of what was happening. Kids that age have the ability to programme themselves into denial mode. The Air India jumbo jet was blissfully empty and I roamed the aisles, not letting the fact that I was a little brown kid with hefty prescription glasses and braided hair slicked with coconut oil stop me from pretending I was on my own private jet.

This was before the days of low-cost flights and holidays abroad; our weekend breaks used to be the typical too-many-Asians-crammed-into-a-Nissan-Micra road trips to English seaside towns for fully clothed chilly splashes in the sea, and the exotic (to every daily curry eater) treat of fish and chips with a gallon of vinegar. So being on a Boeing 747 was as exciting as flying to the moon. I'd get a little thrill whenever the air hostesses would briefly part the little blue curtains that enclosed the mini kitchen, trying to decode the scribbles on the metal containers that they'd slam in and out of the lockers.

I sat down next to the window in an empty row of

seats. Squishing my nose up against the glass as I gazed out to pink-tinged clouds, I pretended I was a rich kid on my way to a private island to be tutored at home in between swimming in a tropical sea and sipping lassi by the pool.

I used to talk to myself a lot back then, forever lost in a dream world. Meandering down the aisles while having an animated conversation between me and . . . me, I startled when I passed another little girl. White, American and about my age. In the easy way that kids do, before they've entered the world of grown-ups and 'excuse me' and 'sorry do you mind if sit there', I plopped myself down next to her. We talked about where we lived, our favourite TV shows, what we liked to eat.

We spent a good half an hour debating the merits of Lionel Richie's song 'Hello', agreeing it was probably not the best idea for him to start by saying, 'I love you'.

We were somewhere over the Indian Ocean when she asked me, 'What part of America is India in?' I tilted my head to one side and thought, *Neither – obviously*.

'Is it in South America or North America?' she soldiered on with her ignorance.

That little snapshot right there represents the difference between me, a British Indian, and someone like her. She had never had to think about a world beyond her home, or to worry about where she fitted in it. Not being the minority in race, culture or religion, she simply never had to. I, on the other hand, even at eight, knew the exact coordinates of my life. I knew that I'd been born in England but that I wasn't exactly from there, and that my parents came from India, a place I couldn't picture but could point out on a map.

~

The night before I got on that jumbo jet to India, I twirled around in a summer dress in front of the mirror in my parents' bedroom in our little terraced house in Maidstone, Kent, all psychedelic seventies carpet and a garden that was more jungle than English garden. Earlier on in the day, my sister, Poorna, and I had been playing with a cash register we were both obsessed with. Although there is nearly five years between us, we had an unbreakable bond, even when she was still a toddler of three and I was eight. We've always been so in sync that it often feels like we should have been twins. We had our own language growing up, in-jokes galore, and would quite literally be prepared to kill anyone who upset the other.

Prancing around in front of the mirror, out of the corner of my eye I could see Mum and my aunt talking softly to each other in Tulu, their mother tongue from the south of India. I couldn't speak it, but understood most of it.

'Poor thing,' I heard my aunt say with a heavy heart. 'She doesn't know what's happening tomorrow, does she?'

'It's hard to explain these things to an eight-year-old,' Mum said, her voice cracking slightly.

'She'll understand one day.'

Reaching that day took much longer than she may have expected. Their reasoning for sending me off to India was this: my grandfather was in poor health and had asked to spend time with me. As I was growing up fast, my mum wanted me to experience living in India. The plan was that they would sell our house in Kent and move to join me within the year. Life rarely goes to plan and this didn't happen. It was four years before they finally came over, and in the meantime I was living away from something all children deserve to grow up around – their parents and their siblings – a separation that I didn't properly process at the time, but which has left me with a kernel of sadness as I've got older and had my own child.

On the plane I watched the sun rise and blister through the tiny windows. As the sky showed off in all its glory, offering up a dazzling display of pinks, oranges and reds, I felt a searing pain in my ears as my little eardrums tried to cope with the rapidly changing air pressure.

My aunt, who was escorting me to my new life, offered me a boiled sweet and stroked my cheek. '*Paapa baley,*' she said tenderly.

Poor child.

~

'Chocolate is my favourite flavour, though!' my best friend, Mark Worthington, screeched as he chased after me through the playground. At the age of seven and three-quarters, during a game of 'what ice cream would you be?', I realized I wasn't like the other vanilla-coloured kids at our primary school in Kent, in the south-east of England.

It was 1984 and Nena's '99 Red Balloons' was playing on loop on radios everywhere; boys were walking around robotically threatening 'I'll be back', girls were wrapped in neon velour and spandex. I was an introspective, bookish kid in NHS-style soda-bottle glasses who knew I wasn't like the rest, but it hadn't occurred to me that I was actually seen as different.

The most profound realizations in life can come in the most mundane ways – like being told you were the only chocolate sundae in a group of vanilla milkshakes. There was no malice in what they said. Like most kids, they simply said what they thought. But as I felt my world stop spinning on its axis for a moment, I did the only logical thing I could think of. I fled. Running unusually fast for someone who thought up new and inventive ways to get out of PE every day, I bolted, face flaming red and hot with shame at being branded different.

The 1980s were years in which brown kids all over England were battling with their chappati-eating identities at home and their Top-Trumps-playing avatars at school. While they were figuring out how best to fly under the radar (was it better to shrug off racist comments, biding your time till you drew in the big bucks as doctors or lawyers, or should you fight your corner?), I was going in the exact opposite direction. Quite literally.

I became a new British immigrant in India, trying to master the art of waggling my head in the non-committal Indian way that can mean *yes, no, maybe, I'll think about it,* or whatever.

Until then, I had been living on a quiet tree-lined street in England, where it drizzled endlessly. People moved to and from work under perma-grey skies, and they holed up at home in the evenings splashing salt and vinegar on to their fish and chips. The next thing I knew, my eight-year-old self was plonked out of an Air India plane smelling of onion bhaji (the plane, not me), into the humid fug of Mangalore on the south-west coast of India. Mangalore is a fishing town squished between the Indian Ocean and the Western Ghats – a mountain range so perilously winding with hairpin bends that during car journeys I clutched a plastic bag just in case my stomach didn't comply with the dizzying twists.

During the monsoon, warm rain-laden clouds slam into the mountains, depositing their entire motherload on to the little coastal towns clinging to the edge of the subcontinent. There's no waiting for the rain to stop to pop out to the shops during the monsoon; you wear plastic jelly shoes, take the biggest umbrella you can find, hitch up your clothes, pray to Vishnu or Our Lady of Beyoncé (whichever god you believe in) and simply hope for the best.

Landing in India was like that moment in *The Wizard of Oz* when Judi Garland's Dorothy lands in Oz and the film goes from black and white to Technicolor. In Kent, we had lived on a quiet road, entirely populated with white families. There was very little noise, except for the ambulances that used to pull up at the hospital in front of our house (where Dad was a doctor). My environment mostly existed in shades of green, white and grey.

But in India, for the first time in my life, I was surrounded by thousands of people who all looked like me, all trying to go in different directions at the same time.

Though Mangalore was a fairly sleepy city in comparison to most others in India, it fizzed with colour and sound. There were rickshaw drivers honking their horns trying to overtake motorbikes, who would then rev their engine in an attempt to regain their advantage. Buses and lorries would lumber past like giant multicoloured rhinos, decorated with pictures of Hindu gods and slogans like 'Horn OK Please' or '*Mere Bharat Mahan*', the latter translating to 'My Great India'. When someone felt like they were being unfairly overtaken, they would both sound their horn and scream out of their window, the sound combining with the general high volume that many Indians speak at, whether they are chatting to their friends or trying to buy something from a shop. A total contrast to British people shushing their kids in public spaces.

Fruit and vegetable sellers on the side of the road would regularly bellow to let people know they were there and had a good deal on mangoes or aubergines or whatever was in season. Recycling happened in the form of wizened men pushing carts collecting paper or bottles, screeching 'paaaayperrrr' (paper) or 'baattlii battlii battlii' (bottles), projecting their voices over the permanent din of street life as well as if they'd been trained opera singers.

I went to St Mary's School, about thirty seconds up the road from where we lived. Once my grandparents were sure I could cross the road without getting hit by a motorbike, I was allowed to walk there and back by myself.

'What? Eees-barraha?' my new primary school teacher bellowed when I told her the name of my old school in

England. I wouldn't have been surprised if teachers at that school had been given lessons in projecting their voice – we were lumped as seventy-five students in large, football-stadium-sized classrooms.

'Eastborough, Miss. It was called Eastborough Primary School.' It was my first day at St Mary's and I tugged at my new blue-and-white uniform as I explained my origin story. I was still a shy kid and wasn't too comfortable standing up in front of around seventy other kids who didn't quite understand why a brown kid spoke with an English accent.

'Oh hair-lair,' they would overenunciate to mimic the way I said hello. There was no malice in it, just curiosity.

'*Niwu Inglend raani yondige friends-aa?*' they would giggle. 'Are you friends with the Queen of England?'

My grandparents, long retired, would nap, play cards with neighbours and regale me with stories of their lives as teachers in Ghana and Ethiopia. And that was as exciting as life got back then.

~

I was happy with my life in India even though I missed my mum and dad and, more than anything, my little shrimp of a baby sister, who was not yet four years old when I left. There were other complicated feelings to do with being separated from my family, but that was not due to a lack of love, but because they are irreplaceable. Even now, when life feels hard, I feel their absence acutely.

That phrase 'it takes a village to raise a child' epitomizes what my childhood was like. Partly, it was because my grandparents were older, which meant everyone wanted to help take the load off them. But then, in India, everyone is up in everyone else's business whether you want them to be or not.

We lived in a big apartment block that had a large compound encased in a giant metal gate, which made us feel safe. The neighbouring kids and I ran in and out of each other's houses in a huge rowdy group, from Aarthi, the littlest at six years, to Arjun, the oldest at fifteen, only ever going to our own houses at dinnertime. We'd skulk behind the buildings where we'd draw hopscotch squares on to the concrete. Or we hung out on the huge drive-way lined with coconut palms inventing games like who could balance between two sides of the building, legs propped up on opposing walls, without falling or pulling a muscle.

Even though my grandparents almost never knew exactly where I was in the compound after school, they knew someone would.

Mrs Rai, who sat on her porch weaving rainbow-hued plastic baskets, was in a prime spot to keep her watchful gaze on us all. Then there was Chotu the watchman, dressed in a faded khaki uniform with a jaunty little black cap, who would sit at the main gate, chewing supari night and day. In the face of real danger, Chotu would have been about as useful as a chocolate teapot, but he did keep a close eye on us kids, making sure we didn't leave the apartment block.

This sense of community wasn't forced, it just was. We all looked out for each other. When Aarthi's grand-mother died, the whole building pitched in, sending food and looking after the children. Whenever my grandfather had a particularly bad bout of asthma, neighbours would pop in to see if we needed anything. There was a collective sense of responsibility that I have never found so deeply rooted in England. Maybe it did exist once upon a time, but in the highly individualistic society that prevails in Britain now, it feels like people mind their own business and stay out of others'. But in India, there was no scenario in which a child might be doing something naughty without a passing adult taking charge.

This is why every time I think back to my childhood there, even though I was torn away from my parents and sister, I don't recall feeling abandoned, lonely or sad. I felt safe. Looked after. Part of a community. This meant that when my mum and sister moved to Mangalore to join me when I was twelve (Dad was planning to follow soon after), as happy as I was to live with them again, it didn't feel like now I was with family again – more that I now had even more love around me.

Whenever I told the story of my childhood to anyone in England, though, they reacted with shock at being sent away from my parents, even though boarding school culture is still going strong in the UK. But they never prodded me about it because of that particular British brand of discomfort where they would rather chew their toenails in public than ask you directly about something. It was only when I spoke to other immigrant families that I learnt it wasn't uncommon at all for aunts and uncles or grandparents to raise children.

The concept of family that most of us in the UK and

USA are familiar with is that of a nuclear one, where the parents and children are the tight unit at the centre that branches out to include cousins and grandparents. But so much of the rest of the world operates in sprawling extended families, and not just Africa or Asia but also Western European countries such as Italy and Greece, where grandparents often live in the same house as their grandchildren, and where cousins are interchangeable with your brothers and sisters.

A couple of years after Mum and Poorna joined me in Mangalore, we left the 'one-horse town', as Mum would occasionally call it in frustration, for the bright lights of the bigger city Bangalore. My mum's sister and brother lived there, as well as my dad's mum and several of his cousins. For me, in Bangalore, my cousins quickly became like extra siblings. Two of my cousins, Ruthu and Ramya, sisters about three years apart in age, lived around fifteen minutes away, and as a teenager I would often walk over to their house to hang out in their shared bedroom. Ruthu and I were obsessed with the eighties pop idol George Michael, lusting over his stubble beard, thick hair and tight black leather jeans. This was years before we realized that whoever he gave his heart to in 'Last Christmas', it wasn't the dark-haired girl in the video. Things like homosexuality weren't discussed in India, but then this was the eighties, and neither George Michael nor Boy George had come out even in England.

'Wait, rewind the tape a bit, I didn't catch that line.' I looked up from my notebook.

'Was it "A crowded room, friends with tie-dyes"?'

Ruthu doubled over laughing. 'What the hell does that mean?'

As we rarely had the imported original cassette tapes (this was about 1986 and nearly two decades before Google), we had to write down the song lyrics by listening, pausing and rewinding. Over and over again.

Her older sister, Ramya, sitting a few feet away on her bed reading a Nancy Drew mystery, rolled her eyes. 'Oh god, you guys are too much! How many times am I supposed to listen to this stupid song on repeat?'

Ruthu and I looked at each other and had to suppress a laugh. *Click*. The cassette player went on again. 'Laaast Christmas . . .'

~

So much of our life was spent with family or with friends who were as close as family. No one called to say they were coming over, they just dropped in. A quick pop-in could easily turn into a four-hour dinner where other people would show up too and no one would leave hungry.

Back in England, though, no one I met had experienced anything like this growing up. When we moved back to Kent, it felt odd to have grown up in such a noisy, rowdy environment when everyone else had quiet homes with three or four people in them.

While it's the nuclear family with 2.4 children that is the outlier across the globe, society has embraced this concept so wholeheartedly that it makes anyone who has not grown up in that set-up feel like something was broken with the way they were raised.

Even though advertising and film-making may have caught up now with the idea that there are many different types of families, government policy and societal structures have not. In 2020, there were 2.9 million single-parent families in the UK, accounting for 15 per cent of families in the country, yet there is almost zero help for these families, with state support rapidly vanishing with an increasingly right-wing government.

I grew up thinking I was alone in feeling 'othered' but this isn't confined to being torn between two cultures. Anything that sets people apart from the norm – be that growing up in a blended family or being a single mum – can lead to them feeling marginalized and isolated.

My own experience has taught me that politicians can't prescribe what a family should look like. Even now, despite the growth of blended families and thriving single-parent and same-sex families, heterosexual nuclear families are still viewed as the 'norm'. Society has evolved, and so must the idea of family.

Growing up in India definitely influenced the way I think about the relation between myself and my family and community. Science shows that the brains of people who grow up in 'collectivist' societies, where the group is valued over the individual (common in countries in Asia and Africa), are wired slightly differently to those who live in 'individualistic' societies (such as in the UK or USA), where independence and personal growth are valued more highly.

Neurologists have found that when people in collectivist societies look at a picture, they pay attention to the background and context, whereas those in individualistic societies zero in on the focus of the picture. Given that what we see influences how we think, we are sometimes operating in an entirely different world from people raised differently to us.

Leela won't have the experience of growing up in a country like India, at least not in her childhood. But being in Spain (where we moved after four years in France) can feel like a decent approximation by virtue of it being a country where, at weekends, families still gather to eat lunch, infant grandchildren running around the ankles of their *abuelos*. It's no coincidence that both Shabby and I were drawn to Spain, and not just because Barcelona is a party town that does a killer sangria. This is a country where people understand that family and community are our foundations. That human beings are not designed to operate as solo creatures.

Leela has never felt like an only child, even though she has never lived with Maiya and Otis, Shabby's older children from a previous relationship. Even though they live back in the UK, Leela has felt from day one that she's part of a big family. Shabby made sure that his older kids visited us often when Leela was a baby in Brighton, and as she was part bottle-fed, they were able to hold their tiny sister in their arms and feed her. All she knows is she loves them and they love her, and she speaks of them with the same sense of ever-presence as her best friend Francesca does when relaying a tale of her little brother Leo annoying her.

'My brother Otis does that too sometimes,' Leela will say, matter-of-fact.

She knows she's not alone in this.

~

The peculiarity of living between two countries is that you can sometimes feel 'other' even within your own family. In India, although I felt such kinship with people who not only looked like me but had a shared cultural bedrock – we took our shoes off at the front door and ate food that stained our hands with turmeric – I still had a feeling of not quite belonging.

Whether I was in India or England, it felt like half of my molecules were always suspended in the other country. Like Schrödinger's cat, I existed in two states at the same time – belonging to both countries and neither, simultaneously. Even though I had been brought up in an Indian household in England and moved to India to live with my grandparents at a young age, it felt like I'd missed out on a million other tiny things that made someone a 'proper Indian'.

In India, I was the *firangi*, who, even when my British accent had faded, would still think about the places and people my new school friends had never heard of. I dreamt about conkers, Wrigley's chewing gum and *Sesame Street*. Annual visits from Mum and Dad brought treats of rainbow-hued pens and fat new notebooks from WHSmith, and chocolates (Twix and Bounty) that made heat-resistant Indian chocolate seem like vulcanized rubber.

When you're the child of an immigrant, there is no

single place that feels like home. For me, England has always been familiar. Hurtling down the M25 past green countryside, stepping into a pub, being on the underground – all of these are signifiers that tell me I'm in the country I was born in. But no matter how much I love England, that visceral connection to home comes only in India or places that remind me of it.

'I feel homesick,' I told Shabby when we lived in France and I was working for the World Health Organization in Geneva. They are based in Switzerland, but we lived in the hinterlands of France about fifteen minutes away. It felt like we were never properly in one country or the other. And feeling homesick was complicated too.

'Homesick? For which home?' Shabby replied with a wry smile.

It still feels to me sometimes that India is the only place I will ever truly feel at home, accepted, wanted, and sense that I belong. It's gutting to think I will never live there. For a brief while, after I spent a year in Mumbai in 2010, I contemplated moving there permanently, but after returning for Poorna's wedding, I promptly got together with her friend and colleague Shabby, after which I knew that would be impossible. For one thing, Maiya and Otis live in England. Plus, Shabby was born in Dhaka, Bangladesh, and India doesn't give long-stay visas to anyone born there (or Pakistan or Sri Lanka for that matter).

When Shabby applies for a visa to India, despite the fact that Bangladesh and India were once a single country, he can only get a month-long, single-entry visa. My cousin's white English husband meanwhile has been granted a lifetime visa to India. In fact, Leela will never be eligible for a lifetime visa because her father was born in Bangladesh. If she ever has children, even they won't get a lifetime visa because they would have a grandfather who was born in Bangladesh. A reminder that the shadows of colonialism are indeed far-reaching.

Bangladesh was once part of India as East Bengal. During the partition of India that was masterminded by the British in 1947, it became East Pakistan (lump the Muslims together even though they're 1,372 miles apart, that'll work!), and then in 1971, after much bloodshed and, ironically, aided by the military might of India, it liberated itself from Pakistan to become Bangladesh. The wounds carved in by British rulers have still not healed half a century later and the countries that became independent from India are still treated with hostility.

We're not meant to get on. An Indian–Bangladeshi marriage is still quite the rarity. Even my father, possibly the most understanding human being when it comes to the happiness of his daughters, took some convincing before he gave his blessings.

'Whoever Priya chooses, we will accept,' I overheard him tell Shabby when we were over for lunch one Sunday. 'But Bangladeshis can be, you know, strict with their religion. I want to be sure you will not ask her to convert to Islam, or anything like that.'

'Don't worry, I'm not in any way religious,' Shabby assured him. 'I'm literally sitting here drinking all your whisky . . .'

~

One afternoon, Poorna and I are hunkered down on the sofa of my parents' house catching up as I'm on a flying visit back from Barcelona.

We're drinking cups of tea, probably our eleventh brew of the day.

'Pri, I've been really missing India,' Poorna sighs. 'It's been so long since I've been there. I'm missing our relatives, and . . . just being there.'

I tell her I know what she means. It's been five years since we went with Leela. 'It's crazy to think we've been away for so long.'

We might have gone back sooner if not for the pandemic.

Poorna turns to me to share an epiphany. 'I think this is why I love going to Thailand so much.' She'd spent a couple of months at the start of 2022 in Phuket to escape the never-ending winter that England seemed to be in and was planning to do it again. 'Being somewhere so tropical reminds me of India, but it's not just that, it's how the people are too – they're so warm and friendly.'

I know exactly what she means. South East Asia offers me that glimmer of connection with India too. Even though, culturally, countries like Indonesia and Thailand are different from South Asian countries like India or Bangladesh, there are significant overlaps in terms of the importance they place on family and togetherness. Of respecting older people and looking after them, even when it's not convenient in our own busy lives. A feeling that, in any community, the sum is greater than its parts.

This sense of home extends to anywhere that reminds

me of India, including parts of Africa. On a solo writing trip to Marrakech, I lean back in the taxi from the airport as the call to prayer drifts in through the open window. In Bangalore, our apartment was near a mosque and the *azaan* for Maghrib (the sunset prayer) was the soundtrack to our dinnertime.

Looking out as we zoom past buildings in Morocco's trademark pale pink and orange with stucco roofs, palm trees swaying in the evening breeze, I see a young family squashed on to a scooter, a toddler and a baby sandwiched between their parents. This instantly reminds me of India and rickshaw rides through Bangalore, where it's common to see entire families on motorbikes, or young men dangling out of buses, looking like they're about to go flying every time the bus takes a sharp corner.

This connection to my motherland is visceral and felt deep in my bones, like someone tapping a familiar rhythm on my arm.

The author Thomas Wolfe famously said, 'You can't go home again.' Once you've left, your very leaving reconfigures the place you were in. But finding these echoes of India in so many other countries makes me realize that home is not always a place, but a collection of totems. And there's nothing to stop you from carrying these with you, long after you have left.

3. Falling Between Two Stools

My sense of self as a teenager was often fractured and dissonant. I never quite felt at home anywhere and life before our move back to England felt distinctly different. After four years of living in India with just my grandparents, and another four with Mum and Poorna being out there with me, we eventually returned to Dad in England so we could all live together as a family again. The original plan for him to sell our house in Kent and come to India didn't work out. So back to drizzly England it was.

It was time for the soundtrack of my life to change once more. For most teenagers, discovering new music sets the tone of life. But I spent my early teenage years in Bangalore in a musical no-man's-land.

India in the 1980s, before the internet boom saw the country open up its trade borders to the rest of the world, was a unique mix of East and West that operated in its own little bubble. Middle-class kids in Bangalore spoke English at school and listened to Madonna and George Michael at home, but also ate with their hands and watched Bollywood films in Hindi every weekend.

Import restrictions meant that pop music and Hollywood films arrived months, sometimes years, late. As kids, none of us could afford to buy imported music albums – if you were lucky, you'd get one for your birthday. Enter the mix-tape shops.

These were decked out like Blockbuster video shops, only with rows and rows of cassette tapes. You went in, and a moustachioed man in tight stonewashed jeans called Munna, who looked like he yearned to be an extra in a Wham! music video, would slam a giant catalogue of songs on the counter for you to look through.

After you scribbled out the songs you wanted, you handed over your pocket money and came back two days later for your mix-tape. Sometimes, if there was space left on the tape after recording your selections, and if you were a loyal customer, Munna would add in a few extra tracks as a bonus. That was how I ended up singing Bell Biv DeVoe's 'Poison' on repeat for the next three months.

The time lag in getting hold of music meant that in 1992 when I started school in Dartford, Kent, I had a very sketchy idea of which bands were cool. Overhearing the other girls talking about Bon Jovi in that den of gossip and bitchiness swirling in clouds of cheap perfume – aka the sixth-form common room – I ran to Our Price, the only music shop in Dartford shopping centre. The next day, I pranced into the common room with a Bon Jovi tape proudly stashed in my rucksack. When the Cool Kids were rooting around for something to play, I held the tape aloft like a medal. Nikki Simmons, who always wore skirts that just about covered her underwear, grabbed it and shrieked, 'Oh my god, yeah, let's play this, this is so old, I haven't heard it for years!'

Even though Bon Jovi's biggest hits had only been six years previously in 1986, in a teenage time-frame it may as well have been some ancient form of Neanderthal rock music. 'Yeah, I felt like going retro,' I think I mumbled. Actually, I doubt I said anything at all. More likely I just felt the bowel-clenching panic you get when you have made the biggest faux pas ever.

As time went on, an unhealthy obsession with MTV and every channel that Sky beamed down to our television meant that I had a crash course in music, film and TV, to make sure something like that never happened again. But I'm still left with moments of unease where I feel like I've made a weird reference. When we're out somewhere and music comes on, Shabby (a music trivia buff who can name you the position of any song from the dawn of the Gallup charts until the early nineties, when he swapped pop music for rave) loves to challenge me: 'I'll give you a pound if you can tell me who wrote this song/who covered it/which singer this song was offered to first.'

In a decade of being together, I've only won two pounds, and I don't know who was more shocked at me winning those, me or him.

~

One lunchtime in sixth form, me and my little gang of friends headed as we always did to the corner shop down the hill. We trudged along in our Doc Martens and talked about the Roman Polanski film we were planning to see that night (*Bitter Moon*, an erotic thriller we weren't quite prepared for – it remains one of the most disturbing films I've ever seen – and in our sheltered little world, we hadn't yet learnt that Polanski was a convicted paedophile). The film was rated eighteen and we were only just sixteen – there was a chance they'd ask for ID and none of us had a fake one.

'Priya, do you think you could go up to the ticket thingy for us and get them?' Kathy turned to me, her mouth full of the strawberry chewing gum she never seemed to run out of, which I always thought was a bold move considering she wore thick braces. 'No offence, but with your accent and all . . . I reckon they won't question ya.'

Ah, right. Another sharp little reminder that, despite bonding over our mutual dislike of Tasha, and Nikki her bestie, who looked down her nose at everyone else, I was still the odd one out. But the sting was short-lived and I'd forgotten it by the time we got to the cinema. What mattered was that they had embraced me wholeheartedly as a friend, while always aware of the difference I brought to the group. You learn very young to label racial jibes according to intent. If 10 was a gang of National Front members running towards you, this was more a 1. But irritating, nonetheless.

These small-scale incidents aside, no one made me feel as invisible as the only other brown girl in my class, Sameera. This girl hated me with every fibre of her skinny British-Indian being. With my thick, fresh-off-the-boat accent I reminded her that she wasn't actually the white Dartford girl she sounded like. That, despite wearing miniskirts and talking about getting 'trashed', she probably still ate a lot of curry for dinner and most likely lived in a house quite like mine.

Sameera reacted to the reminder of her ethnicity that I presented her with by proceeding to ignore me for the next two years. Quite the accomplishment given that we sat four feet away from each other in the common room every day. The only time she registered my presence was to tell her friends how, when she visited family in India, she noticed that rather than drinking directly from a glass, Indians might tip their head back and pour their drink into their mouths at a height of a few inches to avoid their mouth touching the glass. As they laughed, she flicked a glance over at me and smirked.

I know Indians do this when sharing a drink to avoid spreading germs, which I always thought was a nifty, hygienic trick, but Sameera proceeded to guffaw about it to her friends as if it were a bizarre custom of 'the natives'.

Chutiya, I thought in Hindi. Asshole. Despite spending my formative years in India, my Hindi is terrible. This is because even though Hindi is officially India's national language, it originated in the North – the languages in both halves of the country have roots in Sanskrit, but Northern Indian languages have Indo-Aryan origins and Southern ones have Dravidian roots. I went to an English-speaking school where Hindi was taught for an hour a week (South India thumbing its nose at the capital's insistence on Hindi) and the rest of the time I spoke either English or Kannada (the language of Karnataka). Even though Hindi is spoken much less in Bangalore, my cousins loved a good swear word and had given me an arsenal of abuse I could mutter under my breath without being understood (unless, of course, you're in somewhere like Southall or Bradford, in which case best stay shtum).

At the time, I was perplexed by the contempt in which she held me and the disgust with which she spoke about Indians. What had I ever done to her? Now, I see it for what it was – a desperate attempt to separate herself from her ethnicity. That was understandable in a town that was deeply racist in the 1990s, and in many ways still is. I can also see it as the actions of a sixteen-year-old brown girl who was trying to reconcile being different from everyone around her, albeit by becoming the biggest *chutiya* going.

I remember what it's like to be a teenager, so unsure of the terrain you are traversing, constantly feeling out of place; but it doesn't excuse how awful she made me feel for the whole two years, throwing excessive levels of shade my way whenever the opportunity arose.

It was also a useful, early lesson for me that, as the Black American writer Zora Neale Hurston said, 'Skinfolk ain't always kinfolk.'

~

The spoken word poet Raymond Antrobus, born in London to an English mother and a Jamaican father, talks with acute insight into the feeling of being neither one nor the other.

'Anglo nose. Hair straight. No way I can be Jamaican British. They think I say I'm black when I say Jamaican

British, but the English boys at school made me choose: Jamaican, British?'

In the end, he understands that he is both at the same time.

'In school I fought a boy in the lunch hall – Jamaican. At home, told Dad, *I hate dem, all dem Jamaicans* – I'm British. He laughed, said, *you cannot love sugar and hate your sweetness*, took me straight to Jamaica – passport: British.'*

Living between two worlds can be joyous and life-affirming, as though you have a bonus two-for-one deal. It can also mean you feel like you're falling through the cracks between the two. We rarely leave room for nuance and multiplicities when it comes to identity – the world often demands binary affiliations from us; either we're British or Indian/Pakistani/Nigerian/Ghanaian etc. This may have echoes of tribalism, where we once had to pick who we were with, to plant a flag and stay loyal to that 'side' forever. But it doesn't seem to have as much place in a world where boundaries and borders are blurrier than ever. Being unable to identify fully with one or the other country isn't the problem – every one of us contains multitudes of layered identities – but when we're forced to choose, it can feel like we are in purgatory, neither one nor the other.

Salman Rushdie summed this up beautifully when talking of the specific sense of displacement felt only by

---

* Extracts from *To Sweeten Bitter* by Raymond Antrobus, used with the permission of Out-Spoken Press.

an immigrant: 'Sometimes we feel we straddle two cultures; at other times, that we fall between two stools.'

This falling between two stools, being neither one nor the other, can mean always being on your best behaviour – because as an immigrant, or the child of one, you sometimes feel like a guest (and therefore could be asked to leave at any moment). Being the child of immigrants has always meant knowing I had to behave better than everyone else. And it's taken me a while to see that I've been raising Leela the same way.

In France, I would see incredibly well-behaved French kids and then immediately be able to spot the British expat kids running riot, jam smeared like warpaint across their faces, charging into everything they came across with a roar. Why French children are so much better behaved has been heavily discussed, but my focus was always the white British kids.

Whether in France or back in England, I could never get comfortable with my child behaving badly. Raising a brown kid means being acutely aware of their behaviour because you know that they are constantly being assessed and will be judged much more harshly than their white counterparts.

Never was this made more apparent to me than on a trip to Menorca, one of Spain's Balearic islands, the quieter little sister to the flashier Mallorca. We had hopped on a packed plane when pandemic restrictions lifted, eager to get out of the crush of Barcelona and into nature. I'd heard so much about its wild landscape and virgin beaches, and after months of quarantine, it felt like the perfect escape.

Waiting for our Airbnb host, we had a beer in a café next door. We had already sat down before noticing that it advertised itself as an 'English pub and café', which for a brown person can read as code for 'This place isn't for you'. But it was too late to leave as Leela had already asked for a strawberry milkshake. Predictably, she spilled half of it down her dress.

'Oopsie, Mama, I need some napkins pwease.' She was five and still had a little baby lisp, accentuated when she thought she'd done something wrong. As cute as she sounded, I was not yet ready to launch into Mum-On-Holiday mode (though, to be fair, that was the same as being a mother anywhere really as mums are always mumming when their kids are around).

'Go up and ask the lady for some,' I instructed her.

'Can I has one of those napkins?' She crinkled up her face enquiringly at the waitress. Just as she ran back to our table with a fistful of paper towels, I heard a posh English male voice say sarcastically, 'Please!'

Then I heard him say it again, and I looked around to see an older white Englishman loudly repeat the word 'Please' to his wife. Ah, gotcha, I thought. This was British passive aggressiveness at its finest, repeating what he thought my daughter should have said, indicating that she was being un-British in her impoliteness by not knowing how to say 'please' and 'thank you'.

I felt the rage bubble away inside me. Adrenaline raced up through my veins from my toes to the top of my head, a fury that was telling my brain to go over, lift this dinosaur out of his seat and punch the colonial attitude right out of him.

I let it simmer for a few minutes, reminding myself that brown people challenging older white people often didn't end well, and also this was the first hour of my holiday – did I really want to have an altercation? I knew I couldn't risk speaking to him while I was angry. Plus, if it all kicked off without Shabby knowing why, his protective gene would guarantee a police car and an ambulance would be in our future.

Just before we left and my blood pressure had returned more or less to normal, I went over to them and looked him straight in the eye.

'Hi, I heard what you said.' I spoke in as measured a tone as I could muster. 'I teach my daughter manners but she is only five and doesn't always remember. There was no need for making out she's spoilt.'

He blinked and looked extremely peeved but stayed silent. I walked away, head high, pleased I had said my piece.

'What happened?' Shabby lumbered over after paying. 'That tosser say something to upset you?'

'I've dealt with it,' I told him, feeling pretty cool, even as the adrenaline made my heart beat as fast as a jackhammer. It may not be the stuff of knock-out punches, but for someone who was never sure whether I avoided confrontations with white men through diplomacy or cowardice, this cemented the fact that, when it came to protecting my daughter, Mama gonna knock you out.

The vigilance of whiteness against the perceived misbehaviour of non-white folk is constant and it doesn't take a break just because you are on holiday. It annoys me that this policing is something I take on myself. I get frustrated when Leela, even now at nearly eight, still prefers using her hands to eat non-Indian food like pasta or salad, even though in India our hands are our cutlery, and we learn as toddlers how to eat neatly with our fingers. If I eat biriyani with my hands, why shouldn't she eat pesto pasta that way? Whose rules am I following? I fret when she's loud in public places, and as this kid has the bellow of a town crier, this happens often.

But why am I constraining her? Asking her to be soft and quiet when society will do that soon enough? By doing this, I keep falling into the trap of being the 'good immigrant', someone who quietly gets on with life, plays by the rules, never creates trouble.

That rude Englishman in Menorca was typical of a certain type of Brit who likes to remind people of the 'benefits' of colonization in many countries like India and African countries like Kenya, a key example of which are English-speaking Catholic schools. These were set up by British colonizers as missionary schools with an evangelical aim of spreading Catholicism and in many countries have become synonymous with providing one of the best educations as they were more highly funded than any state school could be and had the best teachers.

This is how both my sister and I had ended up studying in a girls-only Catholic school back when we were in Bangalore. We went to Sophia High School, with its memorable turd-brown uniforms (an extraordinary sartorial decision, if you ask me, to put brown people in head-to-toe brown clothes). However, we did leave with a good education, so the terrible uniforms were a small price to pay.

Sophia's had a chapel, and the nuns lived on the school grounds. Some of them taught in the classrooms, but not all of them. Like Captain von Trapp in *The Sound of Music* summoning each of his kids with a combination of whistles, the sisters in Sophia's were called by a small bell rung by hand. Each nun had a specific combination of bells. Sister Maria Agatha was *ding-ding-pause-ding*. Sister Mary Elizabeth was *ding-pause-ding-ding*. Sort of like a morse code for bell-ringing. In the lobby, there was a book that detailed which ring matched each nun, but it was generally unwise to forget.

I was utterly captivated by the system, often wondering what would happen if someone unfamiliar with ringing the bell got it wrong? Would two nuns race down the corridor by mistake and slam into each other, habits flying? (Since our education was admirably secular despite learning next to a chapel, I wasn't burdened with the worry of being smited).

As an adult, it's complicated knowing I was a beneficiary of one of these monuments to colonialism. On the one hand, my parents' goal was to give us the best education they could, and India's Catholic schools were without doubt the finest in terms of quality of teaching. On the other hand, I realize I benefited from an institution set up to brainwash the colonized country with religion.

The visible legacy of colonialism can make it seem, as long as you don't enquire too hard, that there were upsides to being dominated by a Western country. According to colonial apologists, the British famously left India with railroads, Western education, tea, cricket and – what the Raj loves to take credit for – political unity and democracy. Yet the truth is that much of the engineering expertise for the railroads was held by Indians, and India was on its way to becoming politically unified irrespective of the British.

Despite this, so many Indians – indeed, so many people from former colonies – hold their colonizers in fond regard. Former British colonies especially seem to speak of the Raj with grudging admiration – a sort of 'they were bastards, but they knew how to do things well, *yaar*' kind of respect. Add to that those who felt the British helped dethrone the ruling Muslim nawabs, and you get an idea as to why the Hindu Rajputs were so forthcoming in helping the East India Company to waltz in in the first place.

If an alien were to study earth, they would likely be astonished by this phenomenon in which an island nation could travel to other countries, take control of the national purse strings, loot both its natural resources and historical artefacts, rape its women, treat its population like slaves, and still be thought of as the good guys – or at least the not-so-bad guys.

But when you live in a colonized country, you begin to understand how this happens. Daily life in Bangalore when I was a teenager meant many subconscious reminders of British rule, and of their supposed superiority. The British-installed convent schools, like the one I used to go to. Bangalore street names that carry echoes of the British army – Brigade Road, Artillery Road, Cavalry Road. Areas of the city like Cox Town and Fraser Town that were named after officials in the British Raj. These were all in the best, most prized parts of town, as they had wide, tree-lined avenues. In the past few years, India has renamed its cities from Madras to Chennai, Bangalore to Bengaluru, Calcutta to Kolkata and so on, to claim back the old names, but many people (including me) still use the names they knew growing up.

The architecture too doesn't let you forget that the British made India what it is now. Mayo Hall, now used as a courtroom, was named after Lord Mayo, the fourth viceroy of India. St Mark's Cathedral was built to look like St Paul's Cathedral in London. Even the city's best-known park, Cubbon Park, has a statue of Queen Victoria presiding over it on a pedestal, holding an orb and sceptre. (That particular park also attracted middle-aged male flashers who would wait till teenage girls were near the bush they were hiding in before they brought their flaccid penises out like an offering no one wanted, but that's by the by.)

Everywhere you look, even seventy-five years after India became independent from the British, there are reminders that the Queen of England once made prisoners of India's own people. And that soaks in so that Indians themselves are convinced of Britain's superiority and their inferiority.

So how do you find yourself in all the confusion? Fixing school curricula to better reflect history and not just that of the 'victors' would go a long way. Few British children are taught about the murky depths of colonialism and just how dramatically British colonizers caused the entire socio-political and economic trajectory of colonized countries to swerve off-course. Similarly, many white Americans know very little about the depth and reach of the monster of slavery – a 2017 survey* showed that a staggering 92 per cent of students did not know that slavery was the main cause of the Civil Wars.

The consequences of this ignorance are far-reaching. Not understanding the legacy of colonization leads to lazy assumptions about ethnic minorities and the countries they originate from (economic underdevelopment and poverty often come from decades or even centuries of nations having their resources plundered by colonizers) and a lack of understanding of what motivates immigrants and their children (i.e. a struggle for survival rather than a devious plan to 'come over here and take our jobs').

~

By the time I went to university at nineteen, I had lived in both India and England, had experienced racism in England and the leftovers of colonial rule in India, and was deeply unsure of who I was, where my home was,

* Southern Poverty Law Centre, 2017: The Year in Hate and Extremism. https://www.splcenter.org/fighting-hate/intelligence-report/2018/2017-year-hate-and-extremism

and whether I felt (as my relatives in India loved to ask) more 'English or Indian'.

One of the pieces of the puzzle of my identity came from an unexpected source while studying genetics at University College London (UCL).

I'd grown up in a relatively liberal household but, even so, like most British Asian girls, going to university (even if it was only a few miles away in London) made me want to screech 'Freeedommm!' like George Michael in his 1990s hit.

It was at university that I encountered a totally different breed of British Asian girls. These were girls who had grown up in suburbs of London like Hounslow or Walthamstow, or in cities like Leeds or Birmingham. They were Indian or Pakistani, but not in a way I'd ever seen. They all wore black, head to toe, especially on a night out at Tiger Tiger or bhangra clubs. They were mostly tiny and rail-thin. The scent of Samsara hung thick in the air as they headed en masse to their classes.

Unlike Sameera, the only other brown girl at my secondary school in Kent, they embraced their heritage wholeheartedly and had huge extended families living around them, spending their weekends seeing aunties and uncles and cousins. I, on the other hand, looked nothing like them – I was curvy, had an unruly head of curly hair, wore skirts over trousers, and bought jewellery from Camden Market that would sometimes turn my skin green. We didn't have a huge Indian community around us as we really only saw my uncle Ashok and his wife Geeta, who ran a shop in central London.

What was weird is that the second-generation Indian girls I met in England were way more traditional than the girls I knew back in Bangalore. None of my cousins or their friends living in India had had arranged marriages – most of them married people they knew from university or had met through friends.

But here were these London-wali Asian girls partying every night, shagging their way through the student union, who, the minute their graduation gowns were folded up, were married off like painted dolls in a cloud of henna and gold jewellery.

Like university was one big hen party before tying the knot to the past.

~

The UCL campus occupies a prime spot in London real estate. Walk a few minutes north, and you'd arrive at the glorious British Library, which has a copy of every book published in Great Britain. A few minutes south, and you'd be in Soho, home to seedy sex shops and some of the city's finest restaurants. But arriving at university straight from our parents' homes meant that, no matter how much bravado some of the students strutted around with, we clung to the student union like anxious cubs in the big wide world for the first time. This was the home of the fifty-pence tequila shot that could destroy your chances of making a nine a.m. lecture the next morning.

I was there to study genetics, the science of how DNA acts as an instruction manual for living things. Biology had always been my favourite subject and, by 1995, scientists had begun to sequence genomes – meaning that they could now read our genetic blueprint, something that has always fascinated me.

Genetics is a subject that has a complicated past when it comes to race. Its shadier cousin is 'eugenics', proponents of which believed you could weed out unwanted genes and select characteristics for an 'ideal human race'. The idea of creating the perfect race, of course, was what Hitler proposed through Nazism. Around the same time, certain states in the US began sterilizing criminals or people with mental illnesses. All these ideologies had ultimately one goal – eliminating people of colour. Hitler wanted the entire world to be a white Aryan ideal; over in the USA, most people being sterilized were people of colour.

A startling fact I only found out when I started studying genetics as an undergraduate is that Hitler's repugnant ideas weren't entirely his own and had in fact originated in England in the 1880s.

Francis Galton was a prominent nineteenth-century 'gentleman' scientist and a cousin of Charles Darwin, who was knighted by the King of England. He made some genius contributions to science but he also believed that Black people were stupid, lazy and generally inferior. What is worse, Galton wasn't alone in these views, and those ideas were more mainstream than maverick at the time. He established a laboratory in University College London in 1904 and, ninety years later, I would find myself sitting in the Galton lecture theatre learning about genetics.

The Galton Laboratory also produced a journal called

the *Annals of Eugenics: A Journal for the Scientific Study of Racial Problems.*

The first issue contains astonishing sentences like this: '*Science will not flinch from the conclusion, if such be inevitable, that some of these races scarce serve in the modern world any other purpose than to provide material for the history of man.*'

By the time I studied there in 1995, UCL and the Galton Laboratory were radically different. Any thinking related to eugenics had been roundly rejected, and it had become a place of robust, scientific learning that would make ground-breaking contributions to the understanding of the human body. In 2020, UCL renamed the Galton lecture theatre as 'lecture theatre 115' to acknowledge that it had moved on from its problematic history and wanted its halls to feel welcoming to people from all ethnicities and backgrounds.

Nevertheless, coming to terms with the fact that my beloved university and the place that fuelled my love of science was also inextricably linked to one of the pioneers of the ideologies that led to Nazism was tricky to say the least. And it shows exactly why racism is so entrenched, so systemic, insinuating its tendrils into every part of society. Some of the people alive during the eugenics propaganda are still alive today, and if they're not, their children are. This is why history can never be dismissed, and nor can we, as some people would like to do, just leave it in the past, forget and move on from it.

The idea that anyone who is not white is inferior has been the biggest, most well-funded PR campaign that has waged on for centuries. It is a seed of an idea that has been planted thousands of times, in thousands of different ways, until it has become capable of propagating itself.

Even when people don't consciously believe they are racist, these biases have inexorably wedged their way into their subconscious. It's how people who swear blind they don't discriminate against anyone no matter their skin colour can also question whether microaggressions really happen, or whether that person was just having a bad day. How people can have friends from all races, but still want their children to marry a person the same colour as them.

While science can be twisted to support racist ideologies, looking at the truth of the evidence can also be liberating. A turning point for me was learning that tracing our genetic connectedness serves as a historical map of human evolution which reveals the ultimate truth about race – it really does only exist as a social construct.

And this is because human beings cannot be categorized into biologically distinct subgroups with specific characteristics or traits. The genomes of human beings are 99.9 per cent identical. It sounds trite to say this, but underneath our skin we are all the same, and there really is only race – the human race.

In 2021, a quarter of a century after I went to UCL, I came across a book that beautifully articulated this. In *How to Argue With a Racist*, geneticist Adam Rutherford who, like me, was also a genetics undergraduate at UCL, debunked many of the myths of race science. Rutherford, who is mixed race himself, explained how racial differences are literally skin deep – biologically, we differ in fundamental ways that have nothing to do with skin colour. Race is essentially a mirage.

Not only that, although many people might now know that all humans originated in Africa, we might assume that our skin colour evolved as we moved to different climates. But, in fact, genetic analysis shows that extreme variations in skin pigmentation appeared hundreds of thousands of years ago, well before we evolved to be *Homo sapiens*.

Indeed, the group of people who migrated from Africa was far smaller than those who stayed, which means that there is more diversity in genes – including those for skin pigmentation – within Africa than there is between Africa and the rest of the world.

In other words, an English racist and me may be closer brethren than two people from Morocco and Nigeria.

If you're not white but living in a predominantly white country, you know too well the shouts to 'go back to your own home' and the less polite versions of this. These phrases are hurled by people who believe they have the inalienable right to live on a land because their ancestors have been there a little longer than yours.

But our family trees are really just a tiny leaf when you put them into the context of how the human species has sprawled out over the planet, reshuffling populations through migration over centuries. The fact that your great-grandfather lived in Norfolk and mine lived in a small fishing village in India means very little. Looking to your immediate ancestors for proof of the right to call a land 'yours' is as ludicrous as thinking you could describe the universe with only the stars that are visible with the naked eye.

~

Everyone has two ideas of their selves: how you feel inside and how people treat you on the outside. When you're a person of colour, the gulf between the two can be vast as one stems from your cultural upbringing and the other is the way society views you.

This is why knowledge is power. Understanding that race is merely a construct, a weapon of white supremacy that has no real basis in biology, was the equivalent for me of the ritual that many indigenous communities have of burning sage to clear negative energy. The truth about race is more powerful than any lies thrown at me about my skin colour or where I come from.

It gave me a position from which to be able to dig in my heels when someone tells me I don't belong, and to say it with my chest: *I belong here. I deserve to be here. And you will make space for me.*

Teaching our children these things does make our life harder, it's true. We're all so stretched already by so many things that the idea of a cultural history lesson might feel overwhelming. But this doesn't need to be a lecture; just allowing little nuggets of knowledge to seep into the minds of our brown and Black children could be an important way to counteract the barrage of nonsense that they may pick up from others around them.

Passing on this cultural understanding to our children

means we need to grapple with the myths we've been taught too, of course. This may well rattle our own sense of self, of the identities we've clung on to for decades to make life easy. But do we really have a choice?

In *Why I'm No Longer Talking to White People About Race*, Reni Eddo-Lodge describes learning about slavery in the UK when she was at university. She had assumed slavery was an American horror, but once she understood that Britain had a major role to play, she was consumed by the need to learn everything she could. A white friend on her university course decided to drop out of that module as it 'wasn't for her'. Eddo-Lodge marvels at her friend's privilege in being able to turn away from something uncomfortable, whereas she as a Black woman couldn't not learn about her history.

I have a friend in England who, by his own admission, is so white he's almost translucent. An ardent liberal, he's also fascinated by discussions of race and discrimination, and often asks me questions about this. A couple of years ago, we were talking about how Indians too can be vehemently racist and, astounded, he wanted to know more. Part of me groans internally when he raises these issues because, like other people of colour, I don't always want to be pushed into the role of educating white people. But in his defence, he will ask a few questions before going and reading around these issues on his own.

This identity crisis doesn't necessarily resolve itself when you go on to have your own kid – also living a split existence between different cultures. In many ways, it can amplify the dissonant beat within you, so that you end up having to try and figure yourself out all over again.

Becoming a mother can feel like making your way down a staircase in the dark; you may put your foot out with confidence only to lose your balance as the stair you thought was there turns out to be elusive.

I have started to realize that the reason I don't always want to have these conversations is because they force me to reckon with my own thoughts and feelings on such issues, and these are never static. They shift and change with a million different variables. I'm not saying I will always indulge anyone who wants to discuss race at any moment or in any setting; it's my prerogative to have a glass of cava on the beach and talk only about what we're going to eat for dinner and not have to exit the Matrix, as it were, into gritty reality.

But I can be honest enough to say that I don't have the option to not think about these issues, and how they will affect both my identity and that of my daughter.

4. But Where Are You From, Really?

Soon after Elsa-braid-gate we made the bold move to relocate to Barcelona, squeezing through Europe's closing doors just before the dawn of Brexit Britain that would make moving to a European country a logistical nightmare. As far as Leela was aware, she was a British girl who grew up in France and was now ready to be Spanish. It began to dawn on me that, despite her mother spending several years in India growing up and her father having moved from Bangladesh to London aged thirteen, Leela had no real connection with her Indian–Bangladeshi heritage. Being dyed-in-the-wool atheists, we didn't follow religious traditions nor celebrate any cultural festivals; any talk of the homeland was shared as anecdotes, God a character in a book.

Then there's the issue of language. We only ever speak English at home. My sister and I grew up speaking English and my parents never spoke Tulu to us (they were worried we'd speak both languages poorly rather than one language well). People are forever confused by how I spent so long in India and still can't speak Hindi to save my life. As anyone who's been to Bangalore or Mumbai will vouch, a lot of people communicate in English. This is a hangover from the country's colonial past, the irony being that, although India has 121 languages, the language that unifies people the most, after Hindi, is English.

Having spent his formative years in Bangladesh, Shabby speaks fluent Bengali, the language of one of the greatest film-makers of all time, Satyajit Ray, and of the poet Rabindranath Tagore. It is an incredibly melodic language. I really wanted him to teach Leela to speak it. But he had never spoken Bengali to his two older kids, Maiya and Otis, who he had with his ex-partner, Amanda (who's white), mainly because in his role as stay-at-office dad he didn't want to be the guy who turned up at weekends speaking in a foreign tongue. He now only spoke it on video calls with his parents and brother, so it no longer felt fluid and it seemed unnatural to speak Bengali to Leela.

So we now have a brown kid who can speak English, French, Spanish, Catalan and, for a brief, amusing while when she was in a German-run kindergarten, German. Other than a clutch of words like *chappal* (sandals) and *chup!* (be quiet!), she has almost nothing derived from Sanskrit, the language of her ancestors. That language offers such a deep connection to others who speak it; me not speaking my parents' mother tongue somewhat severed that bond to my own ancestors. In turn, I worry that Leela not speaking a South Asian language makes her ever more distant from her culture. Considering she was born in Brighton, took her first steps in France and is now immersed in all things Spanish, is that even her culture at all?

~

On the way to her school in Barcelona, we walk past gargoyles leering down from Gothic buildings with giant wrought-iron doors that sit alongside stained-glass windows in 1930s apartment blocks. Walking the streets of this city can thrill the soul – Leela's school is on the same road as La Pedrera, one of Gaudí's architectural masterpieces – while simultaneously ruining your footwear. Almost everyone seems to have a dog and walking while the pups are on their morning toilet run requires hopping from foot to foot at speed to avoid the rivulets of wee that trickle along the road.

There's something about this age, from four or five onwards, when kids seem to have a new consciousness about who they are switch on, especially in relation to the rest of the world. It's the age that child psychologists call a 'meta self-awareness', as they understand that what they see in the mirror is also what everyone else sees – a dawning of self-consciousness.

'There's a new girl in my class,' Leela revealed while leaping across a newly created tributary. I wasn't as nimble as she was, and swore under my breath as one of my shoes got gently bathed in urine. The quietness of my profanity was not so much to save Leela's ears as to avoid paying her the euro she demands per swear word. 'She's Anglish.'

'She's what?' I asked, confused.

'She's Anglish. Like me. We're both from Angland.'

Oh, right. England. Leela sounded like the Indian call-centre staff who are trained to sound Anglo-American but end up sounding like they've twisted their vowels through a mangler. 'Hay-low ma nayme is Ayandrreeww. Haaao mayyi halp yooo?' I don't tell 'Andrew' that I suspect his real name is Akaash or something, never feeling unkind enough to shatter his carefully constructed guise, so I play along.

More than her mispronunciation, I was startled to hear Leela describe herself as English at all.

You might think you're English, my love, but the world may not see you that way. I felt uncomfortable at my own thought.

'Well, you were born in England, Leela,' I explained, choosing my words carefully, 'which makes you British, but you're from India and Bangladesh too, don't forget that.' I sounded like an echo of my own parents.

A few days later, while bouncing on the trampoline that has taken up permanent residence in our lounge, she asked, 'What is Daddy's country called again?'

'Daddy's British too, but he was born in Bangladesh.'

'Bonglodosh,' she said, rolling the word in her mouth like a boiled sweet. 'That's a hard name to remember,' now twirling around as well as bouncing.

'It's not Bonglodosh, it's BANGLADESH,' I snapped, irritated to hear such a racially insensitive comment coming from her. 'You can say "bioluminescence" so I think you can remember "Bangladesh"!'

All my life, people had tried to change my name to something they could remember more easily. I've been called 'Pra-ya', 'Prima', 'Prius' and, memorably by an ex-boyfriend's mum, 'Puma'. Shabby, whose real name is Shihab, has been sent emails addressed to

'Shrihab', 'Shabob' and, the one that made me laugh for a good few hours, 'Shithab'. While there are many Asians who look down on those that anglicize their names (we knew a guy called Ali Rahman who went by Al Ramone), it's understandable why many choose to do so.

A scientist I worked with when I was doing temp work in a laboratory regularly mangled my name, insisting he just couldn't remember it. After weeks of this, I'd had enough. When we were in the staff common room, I laid into him. 'You've got a PhD in molecular biology. I'm pretty sure you can remember a name that has just two syllables.' He blinked at me like a startled owl, not expecting to be challenged by a lowly temp, especially one who was also female with brown skin.

The idea that my own kid would trot out the defence of a 'foreign' word being too hard to say galled me.

Not realizing exactly why, but smart enough to read that offence had been taken, she stopped bouncing. 'Sowwy, Mama.'

'You didn't do anything wrong,' I assured her, acutely aware children can't be admonished for ignorance when the person supposed to teach her simply hasn't got round to it.

But these signals of her detachment from her heritage would continue.

One of my favourite things to do with Leela is to snuggle up, every piece of her slotting into me, briefly recalling the moment we were once one person. One lazy Sunday afternoon as we lay on the sofa, her little legs entwined in mine like vines wrapping around tree trunks, she wondered, 'Mama, what does my name mean in Indian?'

'"Indian" isn't a language, Leelee. Your Ajja and Dodda are from a place in India called Karnataka, and they speak a language called Tulu. Daddy speaks Bengali. They both come from an old language called Sanskrit, and your name means "playful" in Sanskrit.'

She blinked at me.

'Do you understand?' I checked.

'Well,' she shrugged, 'in Spanish, "Leela" means lilac.' And with that, she was off the sofa and already thumping down the hallway.

I now knew how my parents had felt. Why they would insist, eyes blazing, that I mustn't forget where I came from. How far up the branch was Leela to be able to realistically connect with our roots?

~

With its temperate climate in the south-east of the country, Kent is called 'the garden of England'. If that's the case, then Dartford in the 1990s was like a twisted old weed. And being a brown teenager then? *Oof!* It was a crash course in what happens when disenfranchised white people are convinced by posher white people (which in Britain often means political leaders) that brown folk are to blame for all their troubles.

Just going into a pub sometimes felt like taking part in a gladiator sport. Would I make it to the bar and order my snakebite-and-black (a mixture of cider and lager with a blackcurrant top) before I encountered one or more of the following:

a) Being sidelined. Waving my five-pound note while newcomers got served before me one by one.
b) Casual racism. 'Didn't know you lot were allowed to drink!'
c) Outright racism. Like the time a skinhead expressed an unprovoked desire to 'smash my face in'. Then let out a sort of Vin Diesel gangster laugh, suggesting this was some joke I just wouldn't understand.

Growing up, it felt to me that white, working-class people in our area were the most racist, or maybe it just seemed that way because they were the most vocal. They were the ones more likely to tell you their feelings about you to your face. The posh white folk would say it behind closed doors of establishments you were never invited into. The middle classes were sandwiched in between, making out they were okay with you . . . as long as you didn't marry into their family.

This seems like the time to say #notallwhitepeople. But when you are a person of colour, growing up in a predominantly white country, you learn to be alert to racism and to read its language in a way our white liberal counterparts simply don't notice. To tell when a sneering glance could turn nasty. To walk into a pub on a quiet country lane and immediately assess the temperature of the room. To sense which part of a city it's not safe to go down alone. Your night, if not your life, could depend on it.

I don't recall ever wanting a different skin colour. I had enough self-respect and pride drummed into me by my parents, which living in India only cemented, but I do remember acutely wishing things were different. That I didn't live in a country where so many despised or resented anyone who wasn't white.

I never spoke to my parents about this. I know so many children of immigrants who never said a word about any racism they experienced to their parents. In many ways, my experiences never felt as intense and relentless as the racism other brown kids faced in white neighbourhoods in other parts of the country, where they were bullied by strangers, neighbours, teachers and classmates alike. 'Paki bashing' was very much a thing we were all aware of.

But I was acutely aware that Mum and Dad were grafting away to make sure me and my sister had everything we needed. I knew how hard they had worked to be able to buy our detached house with a big garden in a middle-class neighbourhood in Kent, a step so much higher up from their own childhoods. Dad was once so broke that when he had his first car, he could only afford to put a dribble of petrol in it and, when it stopped, had to push the car home with the entire family in it. As a bodybuilder, he had the strength to do so, but he still cringes at his perceived failing whenever the story comes up. My parents deserved to feel we were happy living where we were. And for the most part, I was, so I kept quiet.

Instead, to cope with feeling slightly out of place, I went straight to the bookcases we had at the back of the house and read everything from D. H. Lawrence to Nabokov, Austen to Melville. While other teenagers immersed themselves in sex, drugs and rock 'n' roll, my escape was books. At sixteen, just by lying on my bed reading, surrounded by my early nineties décor of red velvet curtains, an Athena poster and a pink inflatable armchair, I was transported to different worlds.

Worlds far removed from my suburban English cul-de-sac where the bus driver would shout, 'Where, love?! Caaaan't understand ya,' when I told him my bus stop in an Indian accent. Admittedly, the worlds of D. H. Lawrence and Austen wouldn't have been especially kind to a brown-skinned girl either, but their books were literary lighthouses, telling me that other lives far bigger than mine existed. That there were far-off lands to travel to and adventures to be had.

Once I had grown up, and travelled to those far-off lands and had those adventures, my teenage discombobulation felt far removed. I'd lived in different countries, had many experiences and been through plenty, but came through the other side, maybe not unscathed, but stronger and more confident in myself. It's not that discrimination and microaggressions didn't faze me, I could just handle them better. But being in that French supermarket with my four-year-old Leela wishing her brown skin was 'peach' was a susurration from the universe, whispering . . . *Ah, we're not done with those days, not yet.* No matter how much the media wants to tell us we're in a post-racial world, we're not past the acid-sharp sting of feeling different, out of place. Except now it wasn't me feeling that. No matter how well-travelled, how educated, how successful I was, I couldn't ignore the issue of race when it came to my kid. The world wouldn't let me.

~

The Black Lives Matter movement has made crystal clear how problematic and systemically racist Western society is. And yet, there's an extraordinary push to wash over the murky past of slavery and colonialism and into a happy twenty-first-century world where we're all 'listening and learning'. As if we should somehow forget the horrors of the past and focus on building race relations. But how can we build a future without acknowledging the past?

Remember that as late as the 1960s, Black people were still being lynched. In the same era as the Beatles and free love, crowds of white people would still gather, including women and children, to witness these atrocities, sometimes having picnics literally under the swinging bodies of dead Black people. There are people still alive in the world right now who would have not only been responsible for these murders, but who also thought it acceptable to treat them like a family day out. The darkness, the hatred, the insidiousness of white superiority still reigns supreme, it has simply been rebranded – just look at the rise of neo-nazism and right-wing power all over the world.

The evidence of structural racism is all around us, in the way the police and structures of power treat non-white people, especially Black people; the way that schools fail to respond to racist bullying; the way that people continue to vote for ageing men who don't attempt to hide their evil, just because they are white. I have no idea how we are supposed to dismantle racism when white supremacists are trying to gaslight us into believing it no longer exists. Things have changed in the last century for sure, but the needle hasn't moved as far as people like to think.

When these conversations are not happening about race, they are happening about sexuality or identity, yet all of these intersect. People sometimes hate the word 'intersectionality', believing it to be the complicated jargon of activists. Yet all it is, is what we all are. We are all more than one thing; often way more than two – intersectionality is just another word for humanity.

But acknowledging intersectionality is important because, as humans, we are rarely protected in totality. Sometimes the rights of trans people are protected, but not if they are trans people of colour. Or politicians agree to ban conversion therapy for gay or bisexual people but not for trans people. Not only that, but when people occupy multiple marginalized identities, they may well face discrimination from within their own community – for instance, people of colour have traditionally not been accepting of those who also identify as LGBTQIA+. People who identify as gay or bisexual may not be willing to make room for those who identify as trans.

Unless you are a straight white cis male it can feel as if your entire life is like being in a game of whack-a-mole, where someone, somewhere, is coming for some part of you.

And this messy, chaotic world is what I need to prepare my daughter for, somehow. Teaching her without overwhelming her. As Uju Asika says in *Bringing Up Race*, 'Engaging in thoughtful empowering conversations [with children] can act as a buffer against the shock of other people's ignorance and vitriol.'

While this was simmering in my mind, and I happened to mention to a (white) friend that I was working out how much to tell Leela about race and how people sometimes treat others solely on the basis of their skin, she was surprised that I was tackling this issue at age five.

'It seems kind of a heavy topic to bring up with them, don't you think?' she said. 'Why pollute their minds with things like racism . . . why make them aware of difference when they're not thinking about it?'

I took a deep breath, pondering not for the first time the luxury of being white and being able to dismiss race as a non-issue when people of colour have no option.

'Hold up,' I said, remembering, 'you've told me you teach your kid about global warming. How climate change means our planet is literally burning up. That's pretty heavy too.'

We left it there, but I got the feeling she was unconvinced that preparing a child to deal with taunting about their skin colour was on a par with the end of the world.

~

I have always been split in equal parts between India, the land of my parents, of food rations and no such thing as food waste, and the Western world of my daughter, born in England and having lived in France and now Spain, all before the age of seven, for whom acquiring things is as easy as 'Mama, just order it online'.

As first-generation immigrants, my parents fought tooth and nail for every inch of success and their biggest fear was that years spent in England would cause our Indian heritage to leach out of me and my sister – a worry almost all immigrants have, this fear of losing the essence of their homeland.

Maybe they, and others like them, foresaw what I couldn't as a child. That the cocktail of East and West would one day leave me feeling confused about my provenance. That the question 'Where are you from?' could provoke a meandering essay in response.

I've often envied my parents' relatively uncomplicated feelings about their homeland. While England holds much meaning to them, and they have created an amazing life for all of us here, the land they were born in and where their ancestors lived and breathed remains ultimately home. This means that when anyone asks them where they are from, they reply without missing a beat: India.

When I was growing up, I modelled my attitude to life with my parents as a blueprint – whether that was food, politics or money. How they were is how we become. My parents have always been joy-seekers. They work hard but believe that you should try to squeeze as much fun from life as possible, eating well, buying good wine and travelling when you can. Even now, in their seventies, there are few people who get as excited about a holiday as my parents.

'You can't take your money with you when you go,' is my mum's refrain when we talk about people who are wealthy but live so frugally it's as if they believe, like the ancient Egyptians did, that you can smuggle your wealth into the afterlife.

The only quality that is hard to mirror if you're the children of immigrants is a sense of belonging. I couldn't take on my parents' clear-cut Indian identity even if I tried, and I definitely attempted it for a while when I travelled to India every year without fail in my twenties, but ended up having to shrug it off like an ill-fitting coat.

For us second-generation immigrants, the waters are muddier. Most of us have avatars that we take on and off like a second skin. When we walk into the office, when we enter the gym, when we visit our parents. But when you're a person of colour, there's a layer – your otherness – that you can never shed. The fat liberation activist Scottee talks about how, whether he likes it or not, for most other people his fatness and size dominate everything he does. When he does yoga, he's a fat yoga practitioner; when he paints, he's a fat artist. Being brown is a little like that. It's what people see first when they meet me.

Like the time I went to a friend's birthday dinner in a Greek restaurant in Primrose Hill, North London. It was a warm summer's day and we were sitting on a round table near the window. I didn't know many people at the table apart from my friend's boyfriend. Aside from one person at the table who was Black, I was the only other person of colour.

74

One of the women to my left, older than me with blonde hair on the cusp of turning grey, reeled out the one about where I was from.

'I was born in London, but my parents are from India,' I told her. Every British Asian reading this knows what happens next.

Five, four, three, two . . .

'Ohhhhhh,' she gushed. 'I just love everything about India! The way the children always smile even though they're poor, the landscape . . . you simply must go to Kerala! The coconut fish curry there is divine. Oh, and the clothes . . . the riot of colours is just incredible.'

I've lost count of the number of similar conversations I've had over the years, and without fail it makes me react like a cat ferociously horse-shoeing my back into an arch. I'm not the only person who straddles two continents who feels like this. But, crucially, it tends to provoke this reaction in second-generation immigrants, not to those who really did arrive here by boat.

If you're wondering why it causes such a visceral reaction in me ('Surely they are just being friendly, polite, inquisitive, etc.?'), let me unpack it.

White British friends often describe their ancestry as 'boring' and Anglo-Saxon. Somehow unexciting. The counterpoint to this is that then my ancestors being from India becomes 'exotic'. Fixating on these opposing descriptors may sound pedantic, but what it signifies in a subtle way is that having ho-hum ancestry indicates that they've been the tradition, the standard, for time immemorial. Whereas exciting and exotic things are by definition novelties – the newcomers.

The subtext, whether they intend it or not, is to make me feel like England is their country, but because of my skin colour, it couldn't possibly be mine.

Here we were, at a fancy Greek restaurant in the heart of a multicultural city, and despite me being the only one around the table who had actually been born in London, I was the one being asked about my heritage. This immediately casts me as the 'other'. And no one who has worked hard at belonging ever wants to feel ejected from a group simply by virtue of their skin tone. The only way this woman knew I had parents from another country was my skin colour, as there were no other signifiers, my previous Indian accent now smoothened into a crisp Queen's English. This makes it very clear that when white liberals claim they don't see race, they are not being honest.

It's important to say that, for me at least, people asking after my heritage or offering their unsolicited love for India doesn't always trigger a negative response. We might actually have a great conversation about our experiences travelling in India or some other aspect of the motherland.

As with so many things when it comes to race, nuance is everything. Sometimes, people communicate their interest in my heritage but not that they conflate me completely with my ethnicity. It can be hard to unpick this nuance for white friends.

'So should I never ask someone where they're from if

they've got a Western accent but they're not white?' my friend Maria asks. 'It's just that . . .' She trails off.

'It's just what?' I look at her. We're in one of Barcelona's tiny tapas bars, where people are crowded around dark wood tables laden with *pan con tomate*, *patatas bravas* and *croquetas*, all washed down with a citrusy white wine. Maria tells me about how she asked a Sri Lankan Australian where he was from. He said 'Australia' and she'd followed up with a question along the lines of 'No, but where are you from originally?' and he'd got upset.

'It's just I knew he obviously had family from somewhere else and I was curious. I mean, I love Asia, and I guessed he was from an Asian country, so I asked him,' she says, her words running together a bit in defensiveness. 'I didn't expect him to take the question so badly.'

I can tell she's going into 'but I really didn't mean to be racist' mode that I have seen happen to many a white person over the years, so I try to be gentle.

After a large gulp of my glass of Albariño, I explain: 'How did you know his parents or grandparents came from somewhere other than Australia? His skin colour, right?'

She nods.

'So you are not only making him feel like he's not really Australian, which has probably happened to him a lot before, but you're also using his skin colour as a marker that he belongs somewhere else . . . which will also have happened to him a lot.'

I explain how some second- or third-generation

immigrants don't mind being asked this question but others do, and it can change depending on the day.

'So then what do I do?' Maria asks. I mull this over for a minute. It's hard trying to offer up advice like this on the myriad of microaggressions that people of colour face. What feels respectful or offensive to me may not be to others. It's hard always being called on to answer for millions of other brown and Black folk. But I need to give it a go, or else change will never happen.

'I guess if you really want to know his heritage, you could have asked the question in a different way – something about how you know he's Australian but does he have family elsewhere?'

When people of colour ask me this question, it is different. If they're second-generation, then they know what it's like to be othered, and so a question from someone else with a British accent and skin like mine is asking out of connection rather than pigeonholing. What is implicit in the question is 'I know you belong here, but I can tell you also have roots elsewhere like I do, so where are yours from?'

Similarly, if a first-generation brown or Black immigrant asks me where my parents are from, it is a question underpinned by a deep knowledge of what it is like to come from somewhere else, to try and belong in a country where the majority don't look like you, where increasingly right-wing governments do everything in their power to make you feel like you don't belong.

That night at the Greek restaurant wasn't the first time I've had to encounter that, nor was it the last. Before we moved to continental Europe and the Mediterranean sun warmed my features to a perma-toffee colour, England's combination of pantone grey skies and watery sunlight made my skin so light that people forever tried to pin down my identity. I've been asked if I'm mixed race, Colombian, Spanish, Italian, Brazilian, and on the list goes, all in an effort to label and identify people of colour as if we're butterflies in a museum.

This need to categorize may make the person asking feel better informed, but no matter how non-malicious the intention, it can have the exact opposite effect on the person being asked. When you're at a party, for example, with what you think are a group of like-minded people, talking about politics, holidays and your kids' schools, being asked about your racial origin is disorientating. You feel yanked out of the feeling of community and togetherness and reduced to your skin tone.

Shabby used to hate being asked where he's from, taking pleasure in frustrating the asker with deliberately oblique responses ('England. Okay, Catford. Oh, you mean, originally? You want to know where my parents lived when they were little? You don't even know my name, why are you asking about my parents?').

I understand this resistance well. But though it grates when people ask this, I try to remember where the urge comes from. Having studied biology, I understand that we feel safer with what we know and what we can categorize. The need to put things in boxes is primal and is how we make sense of the world. Scientists have found that when we see a dog, we classify it as a living creature, and when we see a hammer we file it away as an inanimate object, even if we have never seen either thing before in our life.

It's also the reason human beings almost always group into tribes – whether ancient, indigenous clans who marked themselves out as different with individualized tribal markings or headdresses, or modern gangs like football fans or genre music obsessives. Mothers on Instagram are encouraged to find their 'mum tribe' of like-minded mums (although, despite the slow move to embracing diversity in representations of motherhood, these groups often look very similar to my eyes – white, straight, cis, mostly slim and able-bodied).

As humans, we always want to know whether another person is the same as us or different. Are you with me or against me? This is what national boundaries and governance are built on. A demarcation of lines, of what is mine and what is yours.

A sense of belonging and community is critical for our well-being. There's nothing wrong with wanting to hang out with people who think similarly to you, both for support and kinship. But while it may have made sense to be ardently tribalistic centuries ago, we only have to look at contemporary nationalistic fervour to see how problematic that is in today's world. How many rich countries would rather let migrants drown at sea than let them 'pollute' their land? How much blood is shed between people who view other human beings as enemies rather than what we actually are – long-lost relatives?

But while I can empathize with wanting to find your people, the need to put me in a box is simply tedious. I've had to endure years of listening to white people telling me how they're going to go and 'find themselves' in India, dancing on a beach in Goa, bathing in the river Ganges or exploring ancient temples. As if India is a hippie toy town, a bigger version of Glastonbury, where you dip into the healing fields, have a transcendental experience and then head on home to your real life.

What really gets me is the way the same people who delight in visiting ashrams to take life advice from a shrivelled old man in a loin cloth (as if a random person who's never met them is going to be better at defining their life than they themselves) remain blind to the savagery that lies behind the postcard image of India. I love India with all my heart and soul. It's where my bones and blood are from. When I am there, there is a feeling of peace, of being home, that I relax into in a way I don't in any other place. But it's no Shangri-La.

It's a complex country with a complicated history. If I'm expected to integrate, assimilate, into a predominantly white country without a real understanding of the country and culture I also carry within me, then you can only ever have a binary response to my heritage: love or hate. There is no nuance.

~

Being seen as Indian first would infuriate me given I was born in King's College Hospital in London. Though my Indian half is something I was born with – when I do a DNA ancestry test, the evidence of where my genes have come from is there in black and white – my British half is something I've chosen, something I've become. I am as obsessed by the way I make my tea (hot water first, then milk, obviously, I'm not an animal) as anyone born in Yorkshire. I always answer 'I'm fine thanks, and how are you?' when asked how I am, even if I've had the worst catastrophe befall me. And I am so obsessed by the weather, I have three different apps on my phone so that I can compare and contrast the data.

I speak a clutch of Indian languages badly, but none of them fluently. As soon as I set foot in India, people know I'm not really from there. More a Brit in a brown skin-suit. To tell the truth, I sometimes feel like a slightly fake Indian. A *pardesi*, someone who is not of their land any more, as my cousin's husband once called me in Bangalore. He drunkenly mumbled this to me on a night out, and as I'd had my fair share of rum and Coke in me too, I took huge offence to this. I felt like he was telling me I didn't belong in India. And given that I'd had that feeling in England too, it enraged me – where the hell did I belong then? Months later, in the sober light of reflection, I understood he was merely commenting on what was true.

I am not Indian. I am not English. But I'm both, too. A hybrid. There's something about the easy way that Leela shakes on and off her identities – French, Spanish, English – depending on what mood she's in and where she feels most connected. It's taken me a long time to realize that not only were other people hung up on where I'm from and where I belong – I was too hung up on it as well.

Still, it would frustrate me beyond belief when people told me how much they loved India or their life-changing experience travelling in Goa and Kerala. The subtext of these conversations is always this: *You are from an exotic land, and I think it's marvellous, old chap. Not a jot of racism here! And to prove it, I will bore on about how magical I think India is for an hour.*

Yeah, magical, I would think, recalling the forty-hour train journeys I would take with my cousins from Bangalore to Delhi, waking at dawn, while our train had stopped at a station, to watch a man in a jaunty pink scarf take his morning dump by the train tracks, nut-brown buttocks gleaming in the morning light, while the old Indian lady in a sari dozing on the top sleeper bunk over my head let out a quiet fart from eating too many samosas.

For many of the white people I knew growing up in England, the word 'India' would play in their minds as an Indian tourism board advert, a riot of colour as people celebrating the Hindu festival Holi smeared rainbow-hued powder on each other's faces, millions of lit candles during Diwali (the festival of lights), endless garlands of marigold flowers at a wedding, a clanging of bells overlaid with images of centuries-old stone temples. All of the beauty without any of the horror that every country, not just India, carries deep in its belly. There is another India, the one that has the largest number of child brides in the world (1.5 million underage girls are married off every single year), where violence against women is brutal and common, and where inequality is rising year on year.

But who wants to talk about child marriage over cocktails or a dinner party, you might ask? I can understand that. The problem is that when white British people view India only as a gorgeous picture postcard, they refuse to connect with both the shadows of colonialism that still hang over India and the racism that Indian and other South Asian people face in the UK today.

~

Britain today is a different world to the one I grew up in. It is so much more multicultural than it used to be, and we've come a long way from when a forlorn tin of coconut milk and some prawn crackers made up the 'world foods' aisle. From fashion to home décor and music, South Asian and Afro-Caribbean culture has permeated every part of British society. Notting Hill Carnival – started by a handful of homesick Trinidadians – began during extreme racial tension in the 1960s and has turned into a multicultural fiesta with a million people.

But people have different views on how immigrants should become part of a new country. Traditionally, immigrants were pushed into 'assimilation', which meant leaving behind their language and traditions and dissolving into a new culture. Assimilation described this way has echoes of colonialism and the missionaries that accompanied it. And those ideologies haven't necessarily disappeared. Even now, people who argue for assimilation call for Muslims to stop wearing hijab or burkas, for example, and for older Punjabi women living in England to become fluent in English ('speak the language or go home'). There is still a price that non-white people must pay to live in predominantly white countries.

Like many immigrants, my parents clung tightly to their upbringing and heritage. As a teenager, every argument with them about why I couldn't stay late at a party or their insistence on me visiting from university every two weeks, would end with the same phrase: 'We don't want you to forget where you're from.' To me, it seemed ludicrous that I could forget – every time I looked at myself in the mirror, I saw a face that looked unlike anyone else's in my class with a skin tone that wouldn't find a matching colour of make-up foundation for years to come.

But I understand now that being reminded of my skin colour and truly connecting with my culture were two different, not entirely related things. In one, I was viewing myself in relation to a white society – me against them. If I remembered where they came from, my parents felt, the ancient Indian civilization that has endured for centuries, then I could feel part of it. Me *and* them.

Despite having spent years living in India, sometimes the weight of this parental expectation felt constricting, like the scarf my mum would wrap a bit too tight around me before I went to play in the snow. I wouldn't be this angsty about my heritage if I ever had kids, I promised myself. I'd be a cool, contemporary Parent of the World. I believed with all my heart that, if I ever had a child, I wouldn't be as hung up on ideas about belonging.

Then I actually had a child and realized, as every parent did before me, that your theories about parenting before you have a kid are like reading a manual on how to survive a shark attack. Staying calm and keeping your eyes on them sounds easy in theory – it's a whole different ballgame when you're in deep waters. I realize I've just compared my daughter to an apex predator, but . . . if you've ever been in the throes of raising a young kid, you'll understand.

~

The early days of parenthood are described as being in the trenches. Dodging Lego landmines while you escape enemy territory (aka your baby's room after they've fallen asleep) or trying to negotiate with your partner over whose turn it is to wake up at two a.m., then at three a.m., then at four a.m., refraining from launching a missile (most likely a baby toy) at them when they fail to wake up despite ear-splitting screams.

Every parenting book you pick up talks about sleep-training your babies or how to make sure you nurture your relationship with your partner. But what about parenting under the herculean weight of thousands of years of Indian culture when you live in a land far away? When you, bearing the skin colour of the colonized, live in the land of the colonizers? Of trying to imbue your kid with a sense of heritage without flattening her sense of self? That is not the kind of stuff you can easily bring up in baby music classes.

Becoming a mother is never without challenges for anyone, but where my friends were debating breastfeeding over bottle-feeding or reusable vs disposable nappies, I was also contending with wondering what it would do to my baby to never see many brown faces as her visual cortex was developing – Brighton, where we lived, is liberal but not especially multicultural.

How I was brought up – raised partly by my grandparents in India – completely and utterly informs my parenting but we never read about our own childhoods and backgrounds in parenting books or talk about them in NCT classes. Even though, as psychotherapists like Philippa Perry argue, so much of the way we parent and react to our children is a reaction triggered by the way we were parented in our own childhoods.

Mothers are treated as blank slates, pure beings who are supposed to do everything right and put their baby first and foremost, rather than what we actually are – complex humans with our own emotional and cultural baggage that informs every millisecond of our parenting.

When I became a mother, I had to figure out what kind of mother I would be. Every mother asks herself this, but I had the weight of thousands of centuries of cultural baggage pressing down on me. One of the first questions I had to ask myself was how much of how I've been raised do I impose on my daughter? What do I want her to take and what do I want to shed? And if I get this wrong, then does she lose touch with her heritage?

And I'm not sure how you even define being in touch with your heritage. How do you measure it? Speaking your parents' language? Having visited their homeland? Eating the food your grandparents would have cooked in their kitchen?

These tethers that connect second- or third-generation immigrants to the lands of their ancestors aren't the preserve of brown or Black people alone. I know of people who by all accounts look and sound English, but delight in feeling linked to their Russian grandmother by practising their mother tongue. Or another who makes her Austrian great-aunt's *latkes* (potato cakes).

Their heritage too is not uncomplicated, and I doubt their feelings towards their Britishness are simple. But if you are a person of colour, those links are not just channels of connectedness; they are potentially lifelines that can pull you back into the motherland if you need refuge. And increasingly for me, and other brown and Black folk, Britain hasn't always felt like the safest place.

When I was growing up, Britain definitely didn't feel like a place that had my back. But there was a brief interlude in the late 1990s and early 2000s where things seemed to shift, and the country seemed more forgiving of difference. In 2013, when Shabby and I got married, the UK seemed to have reached the pinnacle of Cool Britannia, a melting pot of creativity, multiculturalism and liberalism epitomized by the London Olympics the year before, which was a cultural extravaganza as much as a celebration of sporting prowess. Our wedding was in a cabaret club in Brighton, an underground room that meshed the glitter and raucousness of a festival with the colour and showiness of Indian celebrations.

But while we were all celebrating this seemingly new era, that some went too far in calling 'post-racial', Britain had elected a Conservative prime minister in 2010. This was before the Olympics, but it would signal a shift in right-wing sentiment that eventually led to the vote in favour of Brexit in 2016.

One thing I never thought I would reminisce about is old-school, National Front-style racism. But it's true that in the 1970s and 1980s you knew more clearly where you stood. You knew which pubs not to enter for fear a skinhead would try to bash your head in. You knew which parts of London not to venture into alone. And the English countryside? Forget about it. Now, when I see brown and Black brethren going on Instagram-worthy holidays to cottages in the Cotswolds or Devon, it makes me happy as I think back to thirty years ago when these were often parts of England that these same people wouldn't have felt welcome in.

But anyone of colour knows that while overt racism may be less common by being deemed not politically correct, it has never gone away entirely. You only have to look at how Brexit suddenly legitimized racism again, and while white friends were stunned by the rise of openly racist behaviour in Britain, people of colour knew it had never disappeared, but just went underground. It became an insidious beast that would rear its head when a talented brown or Black person mysteriously didn't get that job in the media or publishing. It would emerge when people who prided themselves on their kids being adventurous and backpacking through India were horrified when those kids actually fell in love with an Indian.

And despite the Black Lives Matter movement opening white people's eyes to racism, as Otegha Uwagba argues in her essay *Whites*, white people who are horrified by racism declare that it should be eradicated without wanting to do any of the hard work. Without wanting to dismantle the very system that perpetuates racism, because they benefit from it. As she says, many white people refuse to understand that in order to end racism they need to give up some of their privilege – it's impossible for radical change to happen unless the status quo is dismantled.*

~

When Leela was born in 2014, I wasn't even aware these weighty issues of identity and belonging were rattling around inside of me. I thought I had laid them to rest in my twenties and thirties and that, at nearly forty, I was sure of who I was and my sole focus was the human being I had just brought into the world.

Those early days of sleep deprivation were like being at sea at night-time, space and time losing their edges so that you never quite knew which way was up, and just when you thought it was smooth sailing, you could be submerged again with no notice. You're entirely focused on making it through the day. Then, when night fell, all you wanted was to get to morning. Not necessarily because it was a misery you were trying to push through – although the lack of sleep can make you think that – but

* From an interview with Otegha Uwagba by Nesrine Malik, 'I've spent my entire life treading around white people's feelings', *Guardian*, 14 November 2020.

more that, when life has changed so radically and you are suddenly in charge of a new life, your field of focus becomes extremely narrow – 'keep this baby alive' – and short – 'let's just take it one day at a time'.

My lifeline was pinging two a.m. messages to a Facebook group of mum friends I had met at antenatal classes. We had only met a few months previously but bonded immediately.

> 2.08: Argh . . . Leela will not settle tonight. She fell asleep but now she's been awake on and off for hours. Might need to prop my eyeballs up with matchsticks tomorrow.
> 2.15: Oh god sorry to hear that Pri. Would walking up and down with her help at all?
> 2.17: Thanks love. I'll try that, though not sure my legs are going to work at this time of the morning . . .

In the depths of this early baby fog there was no time, or brain space, to think consciously about issues as complex as race or heritage. But I also think it's that society treats babies and even toddlers mostly the same, offering equal opportunity smiles and waves. I've watched older white people cooing in front of a round-cheeked Black baby boy, wondering to myself how those same people will react to him when he's fourteen and in a hoodie, even though he would still be a child. How they may clutch their purses closer or cross the road.

It's not that we deliberately raised Leela to be colour-blind, because that's often the unhelpful preserve of some white liberals. Teaching your child that people of all skin colours are equal and should be treated as such is exactly what the world needs. But teaching them not to see colour isn't helpful. Parents who do this want to make clear that they see beyond skin colour. And that's great, it really is. But by ignoring skin colour, you also ignore the systemic oppression that we are all enmeshed in – whether it works for or against us depends on the hue of your skin.

Our home had echoes of our parents' homes: we took our shoes off at the door, ate dhal and rice at home (that was Leela's very first solid food), and interspersed English with words common to many languages derived from Sanskirit, like *bas* (enough) and *dabba* (box or Tupperware). Even though we're not religious, we hold on to artefacts we grew up with. I have a few statues of Hindu deities – a little statue of Ganesh, the Elephant God, that I take with me whenever I travel, and a wooden sculpture of the goddess Lakshmi, who my mum is named for. My husband has a copy of the Quran in his study.

But we didn't actively talk to Leela about her ethnicity or race. I now wonder whether I was reluctant to make Leela feel that her heritage was the most important thing about her. After all, flattening human beings to just their race or skin colour . . . well, that is basically what racists do, to reduce people to 2D caricatures rather than 3D flesh-and-blood complex beings. But in trying not to labour the 'don't forget where you're from' messaging of my parents, I went too far the other way.

The thing is that my husband and I grew up in such different worlds from Leela that it felt impossible to explain to a toddler. The India I grew up in as a teenager in the late 1980s, pre-globalization, is very different to the international hub it's become, with people who live in Mumbai or Delhi completely plugged in to New York and London's fashion scene, and restaurant and interiors trends.

My India lives only in my memory and that of others who lived in a country that would radically change in the 1990s. In our leafy suburb in Bangalore, when the water supply stopped I would be dispatched to an emergency water truck to bring back as much as I could carry.

Similarly, my husband's snapshot of the Bangladesh he left in 1985 is preserved mainly in the amber of his mind, as the country is now unrecognizable. Just before he left, he narrowly escaped joining the army cadets, as Bangladesh was under martial law.

Taking Leela to Bangladesh and India would be to take her somewhere a little unfamiliar to us too, and it feels challenging to explain where you grew up to your kid when your feelings about those homelands are so mixed, so charged with nostalgia but also tempered with feeling out of place.

~

I was embarrassed that I hadn't seen this moment of confusion over her skin colour coming. Leela feeling 'other' and wanting to be what she perceived to be 'normal'. As a science writer, I know only too well how assumptions that some science subjects are more suited to boys radically affects the number of women who end up in those fields. How many girls start off loving chemistry and physics, only for society to drip-feed gender expectations that turn them off science.

This was why we always bought Leela toys that encouraged her to learn about outer space and dinosaurs as much as unicorns. Teaching her that her gender should never hold her back was important to me. How had I missed the memo when it came to race and heritage? Maybe I somehow expected that, as I had absorbed my culture growing up with my parents, Leela too would just absorb it through osmosis. But how, when for the first four years of her life we were surrounded by Barbour-wearing French people fresh off the ski slopes?

The thing that comforts me is knowing that she's not the only kid with brown skin growing up in a Western country to feel that way, no matter how much the parents worked at cultural communication.

My British Punjabi friend Charlotte and I have messaged each other a lot over the pandemic lockdown, leaving long voice notes for each other to see how the other is doing. A friendship that is all the sweeter because we've not yet met in person, even though she's known my husband and sister for decades. Charlotte married another British Punjabi, Mav, and they've got three beautiful kids. On a video call one day, she tells me how her oldest daughter 'wanted to be blonde – her word for fair skin. She was only five and it broke my heart. I was determined I was going to help her love who she is.'

Shortly after our conversation, I read a piece that the American-Pakistani journalist Wajahat Ali wrote about how his daughter Nusayba told him: 'I don't like my skin color. I wish my skin was lighter. It's prettier.' Nusayba was five when she said this, a moment Ali described as a 'gut punch'.

Truth be told, I had expected to have conversations about race when Leela was a bit older than four or five. But I shouldn't have. Children see colour from a very early age, and there is evidence that even babies can distinguish different skin tones.

It was clear that just as we taught Leela to read, walk and talk, we needed to teach her about India and Bangladesh. Their customs and traditions. The fact that they used to be one country. Why Hindus believe in so many gods. Or the way that in the partition of India, Bangladesh, despite being 1,300 miles away from Pakistan, would become 'East Pakistan', bisected by swathes of Northern India, simply by virtue of having a Muslim majority population.

These are integral pieces of me and my husband, and I was beginning to understand how early in her life our daughter needed to know this.

5. To Have or Not To Have (A Baby)?

I first met my daughter when I blinked my eyes open after waking from anaesthesia. The last thing I remembered before diving into oblivion in the operating theatre was frantically squeezing the warm, hairy hands of the anaesthetist, asking him to tell the surgeon not to cut me open until the medicine had taken effect.

'I can still feel everything!' I screamed, by way of clarification.

Having an emergency caesarean section was not exactly what I had been expecting (who does?). I'd had such an easy pregnancy up to now with little more than a fleeting bout of nausea. But, as sometimes happens, the calmest of pregnancies can segue into a birth as intense as a motherfucker.

The day before my due date, I had a routine midwife appointment. It was to be the last appointment and I was fairly cheery at not having to schlep out to the clinic on the edge of the South Downs any more. Then the midwife measured my bump and furrowed her brow.

'That's not right,' she muttered to herself.

'What's not right?' Shabby said, suddenly sitting up very straight. But then, given his last experience in a room like this, I decided to be sympathetic and stroked his arm gently. After he and Amanda (my stepkids' mum) had broken up, he had been with someone who got pregnant, until one of the biggest tragedies that can happen to a human happened, and the baby died around five months into the pregnancy.

There, there, my touch said. I hadn't really taken in what the midwife was saying.

'Your bump is too small,' she continued. 'That's concerning because there's a risk there isn't enough amniotic fluid around the baby.'

'It's okay, baby,' I heard myself say, not sure whether to Shabby or to the tiny blob on the scanner. Then another voice in my head asking me, *Is it?*

We rush to hospital, only to be told I don't need to be induced after all. Pack a bag and come back the next morning. Was this an emergency or not? Was this the right time to panic or should we save that for later?

That day fell on our first wedding anniversary. Shabby and I spent it on the sofa, picking at our Indian takeaway – the only comfort food guaranteed to offer what it says on the carton – staring at the walls. In a fit of interior design pique, I'd painted our living-room walls a dark charcoal. Stylish in a photoshoot, but bleak under the current mood.

'At least it's a good thing she wasn't induced today.' Shabby finds something bright to focus on. 'If her birthday was today, we'd never get a shag on our anniversary.'

'What if . . .' I don't want to say it. I don't want to put the possibility out there, to give it shape with words spoken out loud.

'She'll be fine,' he says, forcing a convincing smile. 'If

she's small, we'll name her Lilliput. Save a fortune on clothes.'

'But the midwife said "that's not right",' I say. 'I don't want our baby to not be right!'

Shabby knows that sometimes the best thing to say is nothing at all, and holds me tight instead. Time is suspended for a few moments. After what feels like a comfortable eternity, he kisses me on the forehead and says, 'Right. Who's up for a pint of amniotic fluid?'

As soon as we went to bed, though, I started to go into labour – or so I thought. I writhed in bed in agonizing pain.

'Are you timing the contractions?' I screamed.

'I was, I just lost count,' Shabby said, apologetically. 'Definitely not close enough together to go to the hospital, though.'

At one point, desperate to sleep but with my belly still distending and contracting powerfully, feeling like the entire universe was trying to be reborn through me, I turned to look at Shabby. He was open-jawed, snoring as loudly and contentedly as a baby elephant. *It's a good thing I love you*, I thought. The next morning, we went into Brighton hospital, to be parked in a room overlooking the sea. Giant summer rays dancing off the waves.

Childbirth is our body's most majestically choreographed dance. When the baby is ready to come out, she releases a powerful surge of hormones into your body – effectively your baby hollering, 'It's party time!' The body then starts the first contractions, the cervix expanding and then softening to allow the baby to come out. It's at this point that you might have what's called a 'show', which isn't flamenco dancers busting out of your vagina, but the mucus plug that seals your cervix popping out. And then the gush of waters breaking – which is when the amniotic sac of fluid around the baby bursts to – *ta-daa!* – make way for the big entrance of the star of the show.

When you are induced, however, that synchronized dance goes out of step. The baby isn't ready for the limelight yet, but the chemicals you ingested went ahead and raised the curtains anyway. Rather than your baby starting the party, your body starts to contract to push the baby out forcefully. Sometimes doctors need to do this for the survival of the baby or the mother, or both. But because it means that the mother's body and her baby's are not necessarily in sync, inductions are more likely to result in C-sections.

As intense as the whole episode was, it wasn't traumatic. But the look on the faces of everyone from midwives to the obstetrician suggested it ought to be. I don't blame them for thinking this. At one point when the pain was so intense I couldn't breathe, I asked for an epidural, but as the anaesthetist injected it in my spine, there was an emergency call over the speakers for her as the only other anaesthetist in the hospital was in surgery. She tried to ignore it, but the call came again, more urgently this time. As she ran out of the room, she looked back to command, 'Don't move.' And there I sat, bent over on the bed, impaled by a giant needle in my spine, in the weirdest holding pattern I've ever been in.

You might be thinking, *Girl, that still wasn't traumatic for you?* But it truly wasn't. A bit scary maybe, and not something I'm keen to repeat. But I felt at every stage that I was part of the decision-making process, that I had agency. There's strong evidence that in childbirth women are more likely to perceive procedures or events as traumatic when they have no autonomy or are not listened to, and vice versa. And women not being listened to in healthcare is devastatingly common. Modern medicine has been incredible in making childbirth safer. But in pursuing safety, we have sacrificed women's control and choice in labour and childbirth. And this has been a travesty. Studies also show that if you are brown or Black, the odds of you having a 'good' birth, where you call the shots, plummet even further.

'I really need a wee,' I muttered, as I waited for what felt like an eternity for the anaesthetist to return and yank that syringe out of my back.

~

One of the biggest myths we are sold as women is that we will 'just know' when we want a baby. Many of us spend our teens and twenties trying not to get pregnant and our thirties and forties desperately trying to get pregnant. What flips that switch from 'argh, not the right time' to 'yep, this is the moment'?

For some women, it's getting married or deciding their relationship is solid enough to last. But for me, and I'm willing to bet for many others, this moment of 'knowing' wasn't straightforward. How do we make a decision that will radically change our lives forever? We've all written that pros and cons list. Debating over how much of our career we are willing to sacrifice. The sinking knowledge that we will most likely be the ones doing most of the hard graft of bringing up another human being.

It seems unfathomable to me now as my daughter will this year celebrate her ninth birthday, but for the longest time I had no desire to be a mother. My ex-husband, Ramji, and I had met when we were in our early twenties and were adamant neither of us ever wanted children. After we got married, we moved to New York and spent our time hopping from one cocktail bar to another. As couples our age started to have kids, we went to their baby showers, visited them in their early fog of being parents to newborns, and then went back contentedly to our nappy-free life of freedom.

Even though I was raised in an Indian household (and many Indians believe that having children is a woman's primary mission in life), I grew up with the unshakeable belief that I would never want a child of my own. Where this conviction came from, I'm not sure. I just never spent any time daydreaming about having a family of my own.

Whenever anyone passed me a baby, I hated the pressure of holding what felt like a fragile, bobble-headed chunk of playdough, sure that I was doing it wrong. 'Aahhhhh, hold her head! She can't support it yet,' an aunt shrieked at me when I was a teenager on a visit to Bangalore, running over as fast as her sari would allow, reinforcing my suspicion that I just shouldn't be allowed near babies.

Even in my twenties it didn't feel any more natural.

One Sunday at my parents' house in the countryside, Mum's friend Helen was visiting with her three children, one of whom was baby Greta, only just crawling. I stood in the kitchen while Helen leant on the door frame, drinking a cup of tea. Greta came darting towards me into the kitchen, a mini Speedy Gonzales in a nappy.

'Oh, she likes you,' Helen smiled. 'Pick her up.'

Looking as horrified as if I'd been asked to handle a grenade, I shook my head. Nope. Not for me. I'd steered clear of physical contact with babies since that time in Bangalore, and I still had no idea how to hold them.

'No, seriously, please pick her up,' Helen insisted. A crawling baby in a kitchen where my mum was cooking on several hobs wasn't safe. *Oh god*, I thought, *I really have to pick her up now.* Gingerly, I picked Greta up, holding her carefully, and moved very slowly towards Helen to deposit her back where she belonged. 'See? Nothing to it,' Helen said. 'Mmm,' I mumbled before running out to the living room, a baby-free safe zone.

This was not how British Indian women were supposed to think. We're supposed to want to get married more than anything else, and married women are supposed to want a baby more than anything else. There is no room for choice or decision. Fertility is so prized in India, there are gods and goddesses devoted to it, entire religious ceremonies that centre on blessing women to help them get pregnant. In the Tokyo Olympics, when a young Indian female athlete won a medal, a significant corner of social media commentary focused on how she was 'wasting her fertile years'. This was in 2021 but you'd think it was 1951. So the idea that I would be mulling over whether or not to have a baby was extraordinary to many in India.

What allowed me to reject centuries of expectation of duty was that, despite my parents being brought up to automatically think that children followed marriage, to their credit, they were never pushy about it. Occasionally Mum would bring up the topic, admitting how having children had given such joy, it would be a thing she wanted dearly for me to experience. She also wondered what would happen if I got past my fifties and regretted not having kids. I had a more overwhelming worry. What would happen if I had kids and regretted having them?

People reassured me this wouldn't happen. They would reel off their most nostalgic moments of when their own children were babies – 'as soon as that bundle is in your arms, you will love them more than life itself'. But I was haunted by the knowledge of mothers I knew who actively wished they hadn't had their children. They were not necessarily bad mothers, merely unwilling ones.

An old high school friend told me that her mother had confessed that she would never have had kids if it hadn't been expected of her generation. This woman admitted that to her *own* child, whose cells had once been part of her body, a child who had made that magical switch into consciousness while still nestled within her flesh and bones. At the time, in my twenties, all I felt was a devastating sadness for my friend, who grew up to be acutely solitary and without ever having had a partner, never mind a child. Now, in my forties, it still seems an extraordinary admission to make to your child, but I can appreciate how the complexity of motherhood could make a woman want to be truthful about it.

As someone who often wrote about health issues related to pregnancy and childbirth in countries in Asia and Africa, I was well aware that millions of women around the world still don't have any control over whether they have children, or how many, bound as they are by cultural or religious conventions into not using contraception. Some aren't even yet women – they're still young girls when they get married and are expected to have babies immediately afterwards, many of them dropping out of school when they get pregnant.

Since I was lucky enough to choose whether I brought a life into the world, shouldn't I make the right choice? And this thought spiralled around in my head for years. How do I know which decision is the correct one? People with kids told me to just go for it and it would all work out.

But that seemed to be way too cavalier an attitude towards bringing an actual person into existence – the greatest act of magic that human beings are capable of. I figured that if I wasn't sure, then that wasn't a road to go down. So I mostly just pushed it back into the recesses of my mind and carried on with my life.

~

There was another reason I was hesitant to have a baby. When I was twenty-nine, I became sick with chronic fatigue syndrome, still a fairly mysterious condition in which people who seemed healthy are suddenly stricken with extreme exhaustion. Now, scientists believe it is a post-viral condition not unlike Long Covid, but not much was known about it back then.

Often, it was like I was living in someone else's body. I felt like a permanently drained battery and could barely walk five minutes down the road. As a science writer I was used to digesting huge swathes of complex material at lightning speed; now, my foggy brain couldn't remember appointments or what I had planned for the day.

Rest never helped. The more I slept, the more tired I felt. The more this went on, the more disconnected I felt from my body. I hadn't been married that long, but felt closer to death than to being a young newly-wed. Even if I had wanted to, the idea of trying for kids was not even a possibility.

I spent the next year trying every medication I could lay my hands on, both conventional and alternative. I tried acupuncture, massage, osteopathy, something my consultant prescribed called graded exercise therapy, in which you slowly increased the amount you walked every day. I drank swampy black potions of Chinese herbs, saw a healer, did as much yoga as I could manage. None of it worked.

In my darkest moments, if I let myself peer into the future, it looked like a bleak tunnel leading to a bedridden life, like Frida Kahlo only without the art and sex. Ramji, my then husband, didn't know what to do or how to help. Mum and Dad were constantly worried and supportive, but there wasn't much they could do either. A handful of friends were a blessing and checked in on me often. My friend Sarah, who was bizarrely going through the same thing as me, was a huge support and we exchanged stories of alternative therapies we had tried. But the others, who mostly wanted to go out and get drunk, were clueless as to how to connect with a twenty-something who could barely walk to the end of the road.

The person who helped the most is the one who has always understood the very core of me: my sister, Poorna, my 'womb-mate', as we call each other. She was young herself, only twenty-four then, but she listened to how I felt rather than try to fix the problem, or ask endless questions about what could be causing it. She always knew exactly what I needed, and often as I lay in bed contemplating a future in which all my hopes and dreams seemed to be evaporating, she lifted my spirits. It's a debt I can never repay.

In the end, what pulled me through the darkness back towards myself were two things. A talking therapy called 'reverse therapy' and transcendental meditation, both recommended by Sarah. If reading those words makes you want to back away from these pages with a fixed grin, I totally understand. At the time I got sick, I was a science journalist debunking science myths and trying to communicate robust research findings. Scepticism was my middle name.

But given that I was a woman in my twenties, staring down the barrel of a bedridden life, I was willing to try anything. Despite its cryptic name, reverse therapy is fairly straightforward. The basic tenet is that you are sick because your mind and body are disconnected, and the therapy attempts to reconnect them, thereby reversing the symptoms.

When there is no discernible cause for extreme fatigue and brain fog, reverse therapy says that your body is sending you signals for you to change the way you are living. This burnout may happen if you are working somewhere you hate, persisting through extremely stressful conditions, or staying in a relationship that is making you miserable.

The more you ignore those warning signs, the louder the signals become, and the more your body gets frustrated you're not listening to what you really need and want.

After just two sessions of reverse therapy, something extraordinary happened. It was like being underwater, near drowning, and suddenly being pushed up to the surface, gulping for air and coming alive. An incredible chronic fatigue therapist I saw identified that one of the things keeping me sick was spending an unhealthy amount of time alone. I worked from home as a freelancer and had a husband who worked unsocially long hours. At some point, solitude had morphed into loneliness. We tell ourselves we couldn't possibly be lonely if we have a partner, friends and family. But the body instinctively knows what our mind refuses to accept. The therapist helped me tap into what I really wanted in life. How I wanted to live, rather than how I thought I should. This is why words are the lifeblood of a meaningful existence. Changing 'should' to 'could' and 'need' to 'want' alters the focus from other people's expectations to your own heart's desires.

Recovering from chronic fatigue as I turned thirty had a profound effect on me. Revelling in the joy of having energy again and being physically able to move, I began running, swimming, roller skating, and even did a skydive. I realized that until then I had taken my body utterly for granted, and vowed never to again. But now there was a fresh layer of worry regarding the possibility of motherhood. What would happen if I ever had a baby and became sick with chronic fatigue again? If my sickness was triggered by the burnout from overwhelm, well, wasn't motherhood the most overwhelming situation I could be in?

Sitting on my friend Rushee's roof in West London, I shared these convictions over a plate of his legendary lamb chops. I knew Rushee – whose two great loves were food and science – through my masters degree in neuroscience, which I'd ditched halfway through to become a science journalist instead. This was years before he married his gorgeous wife, Preet, and subsequently had three kids, but even back then, Rushee was certain he wanted to be a father.

'Pri! Are you serious that you don't ever want any children?' he asked. I laughed at how horrified he seemed at the idea of not having children, but Rushee couldn't have been more serious.

'Yeah, I am. I just can't see it happening. You can, though, right?'

He gave me a big grin and said, 'Yup, I can't wait to have little ones running around.'

I remember being slightly envious of how sure he

was, knowing that for all my talk, I didn't know whether I really didn't want children or was too afraid to try.

~

Cut to a few years later in 2009, and my biological clock decided to not just tick-tock but clang its way like Big Ben into my consciousness. While we were still living in New York, a switch seemed to have been flicked inside of me. All of a sudden I would gaze at a baby in a buggy on the sweaty subway and mentally replace the tired-looking mama pushing it with an image of me. Or on seeing a pregnant woman in Central Park, find myself ambling curiously behind her like an awkward Steve Buscemi character, trying to picture what it might feel like to hold a living thing inside me.

I railed hard against what I, as a woman of science, felt were merely evolutionary echoes of the basic human need to reproduce. A genetic drumbeat passed down through generations. How did I know that my hormones were telling the truth? How could I be sure that the surge of longing that flooded my heart every time I thought about having a baby wasn't a biological Loki, tricking me into thinking that I desperately wanted to be shackled to an ever-needy creature for years, a decision I might regret when my career swan-dived into the toilet and I never had a night out that didn't cost a small fortune in babysitting?

At times I wanted to scream into a void: *How do you KNOW when you want a baby? When is it the right time?*

~

Like many women in their thirties, my broodiness co-incided with my career just having achieved lift-off. I'd worked for a few science magazines such as *New Scientist* and *The Lancet*, and had now branched out as a free-lancer. Writing to extreme deadlines for peanuts was beginning to pay off and I was starting to receive commissions to travel around the world writing about science – literally my dream job. I was reporting on socialist health policies from Cuba, covering a scientific conference in Algeria, and writing about orangutan habitats in Borneo, for which I travelled along rivers by boat and slept in tree houses. This really didn't feel like the right time to stop and have a baby, no matter what my ovaries were yelling at me.

I could see only two options in front of me: have a baby, bring my career sputtering to a halt and be unable to ever report on science from around the world again, or work part-time and, rather than having it all, feel like I was having nothing at all. Neither was particularly appealing. And all the while, my broodiness continued.

When the American journalist Ariel Levy noticed that all her friends were getting pregnant, she found it 'unsettling'. In her memoir *The Rules Do Not Apply*, she feared that to become a mother was to 'relinquish your status as protagonist of your own life'. She was also afraid of the monotony of motherhood and 'of being grounded, sessile – stuck in one spot for twenty years of oboe lessons and math homework'. This I could completely relate to.

Stuck in the holding pattern of baby/not baby, I devoured as many books on motherhood as I could, but Levy's is the only writing I found that distilled the complexity of the decision to have a baby in a way I could connect with. Mum memoirs I read were either attempts at comedy about how devastatingly different the reality of having a kid was from the idealized Pampers advert version, or they were searing indictments of the trap of motherhood. And, overwhelmingly, these books were all written by white mothers – what unified their books was that the issue of race was utterly absent. None of them addressed the cultural expectations to have a baby that a British Indian like me might face.

~

I tried to find the answer to the question of whether or not to have a baby through a data-gathering experiment of sorts. I generally trust my gut but when I ask my intuition and it responds with the equivalent of a shrug, then data is what I can trust, what feels concrete under my fingers. I would oscillate from wanting a baby so much my knees would buckle under the strain of longing, to panicking that I didn't want my life to become nappies and buggies and never sleeping. How could I make such an important decision if I was constantly flip-flopping?

I began by recording the consistency of my thoughts and feelings, as if I were tracking my sleep or exercise. If, over a few months, I seemed to want to have a baby more often than I didn't, then that was the right path to go down. I told no one about this for fear it would seem too unhinged and emotionless. But I couldn't think of what else to do. Every time I talked to my then husband, he didn't seem to be sure either but didn't seem as anti-kids as he had been, so that just left me even more confused. This was the spring of 2009 and I gave myself till my birthday in August, when I would turn thirty-five, to make a decision.

How to decide when my internal weather vane was so fickle? Friends I spoke to didn't offer any clarity, and most conversations went like this:

'Okay, so when did you just *know* you wanted to try for babies?' I'd ask, like an eager cub reporter on my first assignment.

'Hard to say,' the reply would come, making my heart sink. 'We just sort of knew? Like, we always wanted kids and it felt like, yeah, let's go for it?' There seemed to be a nebulous moment defined by either being married or being together a decent amount of time and feeling mostly settled that seemed to give people the green light. But I needed clarity, not a wishy-washy answer, as, in theory, all the conditions were right for me to have a kid. So what was I waiting for?

Farrah Storr, the former editor of women's magazines *Elle* and *Cosmopolitan*, describes how she had always thought she would be a mother, until infertility made getting pregnant impossible. Initially she soldiered on with months of herbal pills and acupuncture, and was about to start IVF when it struck her that she just didn't want this any more, and, as it turned out, neither did her husband. She also describes her reticence about being honest with people who asked her why she didn't want kids, feeling annoyed at having to justify her decision. But, like me, she also found that none of the people who had kids gave her solid reasons for wanting them. When wanting children is the societal default, there is less reason for people to need to analyse their feelings about wanting to have kids, even though by all accounts many people are not actually equipped to raise human beings.

Listening to women articulate not wanting to be a mother felt important. It is the unspoken side of the coin of motherhood and one that I would love women to talk about more, and be *allowed* to talk about more, because motherhood has never been uncomplicated.

Reading and talking to others could only take me so far. Eventually I had to examine my own thoughts and feelings. Was I okay with giving up work for a while and being home on my own for a lot with a little human? Yes. Was I ready to stop going out for cocktails at the drop of a hat? Sort of. Did I want a future where I never had children? No.

~

After those months of wondering, I flew back to England for a quick visit, and by the time I saw my sister, I knew I was sure I wanted to try for kids. We both squealed excitedly in her kitchen, and I remember thinking, *Yes! I have finally made this decision.*

Just before I spoke to my then husband, I talked to his sister about how I wanted kids but wasn't sure her brother did.

'You've just got to tell him what's what,' she said. 'You're married, and this is what you want. He has to be okay with it.' I wasn't convinced I could simply barrel ahead, but I did agree about the honesty part.

Back in our West Village apartment, we sat down on

our dark-brown leather couch. It was summer and the sun was blazing in our suntrap of a living room. We lived in a beautiful brownstone one street away from Perry Street where Carrie Bradshaw lived in *Sex and the City*, to which people still make pilgrimages.

I explained to my husband that I had been thinking about it, and I knew for sure I wanted to have children. He looked at me with his huge brown eyes and agreed we could try. I remember that conversation so clearly. What started out as a reluctant agreement, ended with us laughing about what names we'd call our kids and exactly how Indian we would raise them. What life would be like with little ones (we jokingly called them podgekinsons) running around. I was surprised he had come round to the idea so quickly, and could only thank my lucky stars that we were in agreement.

So there I was with seemingly the perfect set-up to bring a baby into the world. I was married, to someone who earnt a great salary, I'd just stopped being a broke journalist and was starting to earn a decent salary as well, we were both healthy and we owned a house together.

There was just one problem. Two months after that conversation, our marriage was over.

The signs had been there for a while, both of us ignoring them like Brits standing in a drizzle of rain insisting with a rictus grin that they are having a lovely time, until one day, he called time on it. There were tears but no fireworks. And with that, any possibility of having a child together disappeared like a puff of smoke. As so many women before me, I had already conjured up identikits of what our baby would look like. Would our mini-me inherit my then husband's large brooding eyes or my wavy hair? Would our kid turn out to be a nerd given that both of us were? What sort of temperament would they have?

Now, all I thought was why did he say yes to having children when he would soon end our marriage? We have never spoken about that dissonance since, but I suspect it was a last-ditch attempt at extreme denial that our relationship was ending. I had to take a deep breath and mentally wave goodbye to those children I had dreamt up. I knew they weren't real, and now never would be, but the loss felt visceral nonetheless. I was only thirty-three, but already I was doing The Baby Maths.

Women in their thirties will either have done that maths or know someone who has. The Baby Maths is the complex set of calculations every woman who is a) over twenty-nine, b) single and c) wants a baby undertakes. With each passing month that she's single, she recalibrates how long it might take her to find someone to spend her life with, then how much longer before she settles down with them; and if she wants to get married first, then she needs to add in time for that before trying for babies.

Almost every one of my female friends has done this, except the ones who decided they didn't want to have kids. These calculations inevitably become more frantic with time – when you're in your late thirties or early forties, it doesn't feel like there are endless years to wait to see if the one you're with is going to be the one that fathers your kids. And this is if you're in a straight relationship; if you're not, things become even more complex.

So, at thirty-three, as I felt the foundations of my life crumbling, I had to push worries about fertility and ageing to one side because it was all I could do to breathe in and breathe out. One step in front of the other. I flew back to England to my family, trying to hold every molecule of myself together with sheer willpower because it felt like if I didn't, I would, like a dying star, self-destruct and explode from the sheer force of grief I was feeling.

~

It would be two years before I could bring myself to think about babies again.

'Nah, you should have frozen your eggs years ago. After about thirty-five, they're dusty old things not worth saving.' This was my straight-talking friend Taman, a doctor about my age, who had come over for dinner. As I stirred the chorizo and white bean soup I was preparing while she chomped on crisps, I turned to look at her and said, 'Oh, come on, really? I keep hearing about how fertility doesn't actually drop off a cliff at thirty-five.'

She sniffed loudly. 'I reckon your best bet is adoption. Or, you know, do it the old-fashioned way?' Shabby and I had only just got together. Was I really going to be one of those women who starts out manic pixie dream girl in the dating stage, only to demand marriage and babies within weeks?

I spent a few months in science-journalist mode,

researching the hell out of it. What I found was mixed. On the one hand, the idea that our ability to procreate nosedives after our mid-thirties didn't seem to be entirely true, but it was clear that many women in their thirties and forties who had delayed motherhood for whatever reason were not necessarily falling pregnant the moment they chucked the contraceptive pills away.

Scare stories or lecturing women to have babies while they're young doesn't seem constructive. We already know that biologically we've got the best chance of having a baby (and let's face it, the most energy for midnight feeds) when we're in our twenties. But many women no longer view (or are made to view) having a baby as their only mission in life. We want careers, we want to travel, to go out and dance in the early hours of the morning, to see how far our dreams can take us. Why not? Men have had this freedom for centuries.

The truth is that no matter how many female world leaders, astronauts and neurosurgeons we have, for mothers, parenting remains the Sisyphean task that will dominate our lives (laundry never finished, an exercise plan never fully executed, cupboards never properly sorted) in a way it never really does for fathers.

Many women I know in their twenties have told me they can't take care of a pot plant, let alone look after a baby. They're right to feel nervous because even in the most equal relationships I know, it's the mothers who ultimately shoulder the most responsibility for their child's welfare. No doubt some fathers would take umbrage at this but I don't believe fathers obsess in the same way as mothers at needing to know where their kids are at all times. Of worrying in the early hours of the morning or late at night – the time when no rational thoughts are possible – about things that might happen to their kid. It never ends, this feeling like you're taking care of your heart walking around outside of your body.

For many of us, it takes a while to feel ready enough for this lifelong responsibility. 'It's just a design flaw that, at the exact moment so many of us finally feel mature enough to take care of someone beside ourselves, the body's like: "I'm out,"' Levy says.*

I don't know any mothers who have felt entirely at peace with the compromise struck between having a baby and . . . everything else in life. How long do we push for promotions at work before stepping off the treadmill, a move that we know will likely damage our careers? When is the right time to freeze our eggs and will doing so mean we've officially given up hope of finding The One? How much travelling and life experience is 'enough' before we are ready to surrender our bodies and souls to rearing babies?

~

In my more philosophical moments, I marvel at the extreme unlikelihood that any of us are born at all. How extraordinary it is that you and I exist in the world today. That one tiny sperm beats millions of others to swim up

* From an article by Hadley Freeman, 'All my friends had some nightmare experience trying to get pregnant. My story took the cake', *Guardian*, 11 March 2017.

the cervix to reach the prize is a biological miracle. And any combination of that egg and another sperm would make a different human being. Even when the egg does get fertilized by the sperm, the genes that will make you are reshuffled, dealing you the specific genetic deck of cards you are born with. A different shuffle and you could be a very different person.

Consider also the hundreds of life events that have to happen for any of us to be born. Shabby and I had met a few times before we got together as he and my sister used to work with each other, but we hadn't been single at the same time. It was only after I got divorced and was single that I bumped into Shabby, now also single, at my sister's wedding. He'd cheekily asked Poorna for a plus one to her wedding to bring a current squeeze, to which she told him to jog on as he changed girlfriends in those days as often as most people change their underwear. Had he come to the wedding with even a casual date, I'd have steered clear and we'd never have connected.

Then there's what happened when the subject of kids came up by accident. He was leaving the Notting Hill apartment where I rented a room, late for work, and we were having a quick coffee and a croissant on the front stoop, looking on to the leafy street, watching red double-decker buses whoosh past, packed full of commuters.

Shabby is an amazing cook and I was saying something about how 'if I ever had a boy, I would make sure he knew his way around a kitchen too'. I was talking pretty vaguely and not really referring to having kids with him specifically as we'd only been dating for a couple of months.

I'd been gazing at him in profile, long eyelashes, aquiline nose and full lips. He turned to look at me. 'I thought you never wanted kids? I'm pretty sure that's what your sister said.'

'Oh, yeah. That was true for a long time but part of the reason Ramji and I broke up is he didn't really want kids and I did.'

Shabby looked surprised. 'So you want them, then?'

'Well, I wasn't thinking about right now, but one day, yes,' I replied, adding, 'I thought you were Super Dad and wanted more?'

'Nope, I'm so happy I am past the nappies and sleepless nights. My kids are little people I get to play with and that's so much better.'

I hadn't planned to have this conversation so early on. We were still in the glorious early dating phase of trips to the cinema in Notting Hill, where we'd sneak in a bottle of wine, Saturday nights dancing all night, long Sunday lunchtime pub dates with a pile of newspapers. It had been nothing but fun and I had no plans to give him this ultimatum, but now that the topic had arisen, I had to be honest. I said as gently as I could that if we had to part ways because of this there would be no hard feelings, but that for me it was non-negotiable. I was thirty-five and felt I needed to be with someone who at least wanted children, even if we waited to have them.

A couple of weeks later, we went to a party for Bonfire Night, that odd English event in early November to commemorate Guy Fawkes trying to blow up Parliament with explosives, which is now celebrated with fireworks and a lot of alcohol. As we watched fireworks set the sky alight, Shabby put his arm around me and whispered. 'Listen, Pri, I've been thinking. I want to be with you. If you want us to try for kids one day, then okay. I'm in.'

We got married two years later and Leela was born the day after our first wedding anniversary. I may have taken a long time to figure out whether or not I wanted children, even risking not being able to, but I'm glad I did.

The second I laid eyes on her and fell in love in a way I never knew was possible, knowing she'd have my heart and soul forever, I was glad I hadn't rushed that decision.

My Leela had been worth waiting for.

~

As it turned out, once we decided to try for a baby (though in reality you can't *try* to get pregnant any more than you can *try* to fall in love), we didn't need to wait long at all.

A few months after Shabby and I married, I was on a trip to Mexico with my sister and our friend Mal. We were staying in Tulum, and spent our days doing very little but soaking up the sun on the white sand, drinking mojitos and dipping in and out of the gorgeous beachside places. In one of these hotels that had huge sunbeds with billowing white canvases to keep out the sun, I saw a notice announcing that there would be a *temezcal* ceremony the following day. It promised to clear out old energies and make way for new ones. As a newly-wed with a divorce in my back pocket, that felt like exactly what I needed as something was stopping me from moving forward in my new life.

A Mayan sweat lodge is not the best place for an identity crisis. It's hotter than the sun, you're not wearing many clothes and there's a lot of chanting.

Nevertheless, here I was on a beach on the east coast of the Yucatan Peninsula, which nestles the Caribbean, in the middle of this cleansing ceremony, coming to grips with a conflict between my head and heart. I was happy about being married again, but it felt like the ghosts of my old life still haunted me. I wasn't sure how to embrace everything I wanted to dive headfirst into without slipping free of those memories. A group of us huddled together in a wooden igloo-shaped hut with volcanic rocks in the centre, over which water is poured to create steam. The outside is sealed with blankets so that it's dark except for the firelight, and there is no ventilation. Once inside, your body temperature can soar to 40°C.

And so it was in this sweat lodge, sitting bum cheek to bum cheek with seven strangers, nearly a year before I had Leela and five years before Leela's own confusion over her identity, I had a mini crisis of my own.

The purpose of the *temezcal* was to shake off things that were holding us back and see what we wanted more clearly. Having got married for the second time, I wanted to shed the snakeskin of my old life in which I was someone else's wife with different hopes and dreams.

In my first marriage, I was still to some extent defined by the person I was with. As Oprah might say, I hadn't learnt to 'step into my power'. For instance, when my ex-husband, Ramji, got an offer to move to New York with his company, I gave up my own work as an editor at *New Scientist* magazine, despite the fact that I loved it and it is a dream job for many science journalists. This is not to say that Ramji pressured me to go – I was just as keen as he was to zip about Manhattan drinking cosmopolitans – but, looking back, it's clear I gave up my goals too easily.

I've been a lifelong feminist – my mum always made sure my sister and I knew we were equal to boys in every way – but in my twenties, like many other young women, I was drip-fed the narrative that being with a man and getting married was our life's goal. If you had confronted me then with that truth, I would have been horrified. I believed my contribution to the world was just as important as any man. Yet subconscious beliefs meant I didn't always behave that way.

If I look at the evidence – that I gave up my career and earning potential to move halfway across the world with my then husband – I can't help but think I didn't prioritize my career and my personal goals enough. It is not a comfortable feeling to dissect, but I felt like I'd be taken care of and subconsciously held out hope that I would have children and so, maybe, my career wasn't as important.

By the time I was experiencing the *temezcal*, I had become a cynical science hack, more prone to using logic than a ritual to work through problems. I don't know whether I've always been rational and therefore drawn to working in science, or the other way round – that working in an evidence-based discipline has made me question things; probably a bit of both. Indians love anything faith-based, whether that's religion, astrology or homeopathy, and my mother and I disagree over all three.

When we were still living in India, my mum's older sister, Meera, started studying astrology with a guru. In the UK that might have seemed like an unusual field of study, but in India, your horoscope and the alignment of the stars govern everything. Anything you do of importance – whether it's opening a new business, getting married or even going to an interview – has to be done during an auspicious time, when presumably the fates are smiling down on you.

One morning in our apartment in Bangalore when I was fifteen, Mum came into the bedroom I shared with my sister and told us we were going to the wedding of the daughter of a family friend. That neither me nor my sister had any clue as to who the bride was didn't matter, given that Indian weddings are huge sprawling affairs with hundreds, sometimes thousands of people. The kicker was that the actual ceremony was going to take place at night. At 11.33 p.m. to be precise.

'That is so weird, Mum,' I said. 'Will their marriage really fail if they don't have the ceremony at that time?'

'Well, your father and I got married at an auspicious time, and we have been together for nearly two decades.'

Fair point. And by now, they have been together for nearly half a century. But I still maintain that is because of the effort they put into their relationship, rather than an alignment of big exploding balls of hot gas in space.

We sat through that night-time ceremony, the bride and groom walking around the fire seven times (the *saptapadi* or seven steps), their clothes tied to each other to represent their eternal bond. My eyelids drooped as the priest continued to chant in Sanskrit until one a.m. The sound of Sanskrit is incredibly soothing, especially when recited in that slightly sing-song voice of prayers, and I was fighting sleep. What jolted me out of my trance was hearing Madonna's 'Express Yourself' pumped out through a scratchy sound system. The groom's friends were clearly impatient that the ceremony was dragging on and had decided to get the party started.

Madonna purred through the speakers about believing in love.

Maybe I'm dreaming, I thought sleepily. I pulled the *dupatta* of my *lengha* around me. With its tight bodice and full sequinned skirt, a *lengha* wasn't the comfiest outfit, but the shawl was soft, and I nestled into my cousin sitting next to me.

Despite the queen of pop's instructions not to go for second best (or maybe because of that?), the marriage didn't last. Even though the wedding took place at the most auspicious time.

I was never trying to be awkward or contrary in pointing out the lack of logic in the idea of auspicious times or astrology. It was just an impossibility for me to believe in something that seemed to have no basis in reality, and my brain constantly offered up counterarguments. Steve Jobs and Bill Gates were unlikely to have consulted their horoscopes before setting up the most successful businesses in the world, I would argue.

The irony wasn't lost on me that, despite my vocal lack of belief in anything superstitious or ritualistic, I was sitting inside a stone hut in Mexico sweating like never before, casting my wishes out to the universe.

As the shaman threw handfuls of sage on to the fire, the chemical reaction between the flames and herbs made it hiss and splutter, sending clouds of earthy odours into the air of the *temezcal*. He took us through the ceremony in which we invoked the four elements of fire, earth, wind and water.

I fretted: How much of my past self do I shed? Isn't she still part of me now? Do we scorch the earth and start again? Can you ever really leave your past behind and should you even try to?

The crisis wasn't solely about my culture and heritage but that's the thing about the strand of identity that comes from other lands – it's one piece of yarn tangled up with everything else that defines who we are. By leaving some of these threads behind, I feared I might come entirely unravelled in the process.

The shaman asked each of us in the circle to take it in turns to sing a song or recite some poetry and then voice our deepest wish either to ourselves or out loud. The idea being, I guess, that what is said in a sweat lodge stays in the sweat lodge. *There's no way in hell I'm singing,*

I thought. What would I even sing? The only songs I knew all the words to were either Madonna (I had memorized every word to every song on her *True Blue* album) or George Michael (anything he has ever written), neither of which seemed suitable for a solemn ceremony. But no one else had my level of British embarrassment.

A tall German man to my left quoted a few lines of the poet Rilke and said that he wanted to change career, seeing as he felt stuck in his current job. Next, a young woman to his left sang a sweet folk song. Then it was my turn. I realized with crystal clarity why I wanted to sweep away any emotional or mental clutter, to spring-clean my entire being: I really wanted to clear the way for a baby.

But I also wondered whether it was possible given everything I had been through, from chronic fatigue to divorce. The flames of those experiences had eaten up any vestiges of pretence that I could control my life and I had clawed my way through so much pain and grief to come out the other side. Could I really admit to myself how much I wanted to have a baby? What if we tried and failed? What if we had to go through IVF? I had never even allowed myself to say these words out loud, to state my heart's desire so strongly.

Though I felt it so clearly, there was a part of me wondering whether I was unintentionally meeting age-old Indian expectations of getting married and having kids – even though I had got divorced, sans baby, along the way. I'd spent years telling myself I didn't want to have kids, and that I was happy writing and travelling the world. Who would I be if I became a mother?

In my turmoil I didn't even see the irony that while I would never in a million years have gone through an Indian prayer ceremony to have a baby (and you won't be surprised to hear, there are many), I was happy to take part in an ancient Mayan one. Oh god, despite my skin colour, had I become a smug Westerner seeking ancient healing ceremonies to 'find myself'?

The chanting grew to a crescendo and now the shaman was asking us to get up and run into the ocean as a final symbolic gesture of cleansing. The Caribbean was as warm as I'd been expecting and, as I swam, I gazed up at what seemed like millions of stars. As ever, my brain was whirring, thinking about how the light from the farthest visible star has travelled four billion years to reach us. And now it was shining down on our little blue planet. Then my heart shoved my brain aside and took over, allowing emotion to triumph. I started crying. Huge, racking sobs that made the shaman walk over to me.

'What are you feeling?' he asked gently.

Chest still heaving, I managed to explain that I had no idea why, all of a sudden, the longing for a child was weighing so heavily on me that, despite everything I had achieved in my life, my goals had somehow converged on becoming a mother.

'*Ay chica*. You're trying to rationalize such a . . . such a primal urge. Wanting a child doesn't cancel out any other dreams. Becoming a mother doesn't mean you can't be anything else. Do you always try and force logic on to every decision? Everything must always be so . . . rational?'

My tears had mostly been washed away by the seawater, and we were now sitting side by side on the sand.

'Well, I'm a science writer,' I replied defensively. 'It's how I make sense of the world.'

And I also thought, a little huffily, *Why is being rational such a bad thing?*

'Okay, look up,' he said, pointing at the sky above.

I tilted my head upwards and saw big, fat stars looking like they were too heavy for the heavens to contain, as if at any moment they would tumble from the inky black sky. There were constellations different to the ones I was used to looking at in England. On this side of the planet, I saw Lupus (the wolf) and Corvus (the crow).

The shaman said softly, 'That's the universe out there. We came from her. We are her children. Ask her for what you want. If it's for you, it won't pass you by.'

For once, I didn't question it.

I shut my eyes and asked, hoped, prayed. For a little baby. For me to be a good mother. For us to be happy.

A month later, I was pregnant.

6. How Not To Be a Wicked Stepmother

One Christmas a few years ago I sat down with my family to watch a Hollywood film called *Blended*, starring Adam Sandler and Drew Barrymore. We were at the stage of the celebrations where we had eaten and drunk way too much, but couldn't help squeeze in another mouthful of mince pie or rustle around in the Quality Street box to see if one of our favourites was still there (mine is the toffee penny and I will fight anyone who disagrees). The film itself was nothing Oscar-worthy, and as it was set in a safari park hotel in South Africa, it made me faintly queasy with the representations of Africans (treated as a homogenous group rather than a diverse continent) clowning around for white people's benefit. That aside, to this day I think the character Drew Barrymore plays in this film is probably one of the only positive on-screen representations of a stepmother I've seen.

Disney films are the worst offenders in perpetuating the trope of evil stepmother. Many of them – *Cinderella*, *Snow White* and *Sleeping Beauty* – were based on the Grimm fairy tales I grew up with that all see the protagonist's biological mother either killed or dead already, and replaced by a Wicked Stepmother. A Disney executive once said in an interview that one reason for this is that in a short children's film the quickest way to introduce jeopardy for the child protagonist is to kill the mother so that the child's foundations are shaken.

By the time I got together with Shabby, his kids, Maiya and Otis, were fourteen and seven, and the bad rap step-mothers had kept playing on my mind. Given an estimated one in three families in Britain is a blended family, it is surprising to realize that, as a society, we don't talk much about what it is like either to be a stepchild or a step-parent.

This is one of the most seismic shifts in family life in the past few decades, yet there is little to no representation of this type of family in any media or any cultural discussion of how parenting needs to evolve. Step-parents often have zero legal rights, no matter their responsibilities in raising a child. Which means that if a blended family breaks up, the step-parent has no legal right to ever see their stepkids again, even though they may have helped raise those children from babies or toddlers.

This confusion and lack of clarity have consequences. Parental separation and divorce rates are higher in step-families. What's more, when blended families have different races within them, the way they're talked about in the media is very much in contrast to that of white families. Black families in particular tend to be targeted in the rhetoric of 'broken Britain', where any family that doesn't fit the norm of white, heterosexual parents with 2.4 kids is viewed as being different.

There's another issue that affects any type of family

(whether they be biologically related, blended or adoptive) that has a mix of skin tones. Black or brown parents with light-skinned or white children are often viewed with suspicion or confusion. In *Bringing Up Race*, Uju Asika talks about how, when her son was small, he was so light-skinned that she was constantly asked whether she was babysitting for a friend. Maiya and Otis, both being a browner shade of beige, had many assume that their mum, Amanda, was their nanny.

This is offensive and upsetting, and can also have serious consequences. There are many instances where people have called the police on a dark-skinned parent (Black men face this often) when they are with their child who happens to be light-skinned, putting them in the humiliating position of having to be ready at all times to prove their parenthood.

It further exacerbates the constant questioning of people of colour – we are often asked to justify why we are in a certain place. The British film-maker and writer Kevin Morosky has talked about how he is often questioned in first-class sections on planes, as if he couldn't possibly have the financial means to be there, the air steward directing him towards economy as if Morosky was somehow confused. None of the white first-class passengers are ever questioned, needless to say. This goes for so much of society, where brown and Black folk have reported being asked for ID in members' clubs and expensive hotels. Back when Shabby was the editor-in-chief of a wedding magazine and rocked up to the counter of a five-star hotel only to be mistaken for a delivery guy (though, to be fair, those were the days before he met me and used to carry a supermarket bag for life as an overnight bag), he took great pleasure in informing them he was staying in the penthouse suite as a travel reviewer.

When you're not white, the constant justification of your very self, your right to exist and to live with joy, can be exhausting. On top of that, when you are playing at the park or on the train with the child you carried inside you, who you birthed, stayed up with when they had a fever, responded to 1.5 million times when they called 'Mama', and then a total stranger asks you to prove you are their parent? Exhausting doesn't even cover it.

~

The lack of conversation around mixed-race, blended families and step-parenting as a whole means that when I was to become a stepmother, I had no idea how to be one. How much of a role should I play in their lives? Do I tell them off if they've done something wrong? How much am I responsible for their well-being? And when it comes to helping raise kids of a different ethnicity – what with them being part English and part Bangladeshi – how do I leave my own baggage at the door and not laden them with it?

There is woefully little research on blended families and the relationships between step-parents and stepchildren, but evidence from step-parenting associations suggests that it works best when step-parents spend several months building an 'emotionally non-threatening' relationship with their new stepkids, before trying to set rules and be directly involved in decision-making and discipline. But even this research didn't exist a decade ago when I became a step-parent.

So without anything to guide me, I had to sit down and think hard about what my role should look like. Maiya and Otis weren't living with us, so I wouldn't have day-to-day parenting issues. Shabby offered zero guidelines to me other than he wanted us all to get on.

'Just see them as people,' he simply said. 'If they're dicks, treat them like dicks,' before confidently adding, 'They're not dicks.'

He was right. As well as being teen popstar attractive, they both tick all the boxes on the good person sheet. Funny, fun, creative, caring freethinkers who know what they stand for. They had, however, been stung before with women Shabby had dated.

In a monumental single dad faux pas, Shabby had introduced them to not one but two girlfriends after splitting with their mother, one of whom was thirteen years younger than Shabby. This relationship, which had an on/off setting for five years, and was by all accounts fractured to the point of toxic, heaped on to the kids a level of drama both Amanda and Shabby had promised each other they'd avoid.

If I were Maiya or Otis, I thought, how would I want my father's new partner to behave towards me? I would want my hypothetical stepmother to be someone I could look to for advice or help, who would never try to take the place of my mother. Above all, if I were a kid, I would have hated it if my new stepmum had interfered with my relationship with my father in any way. In the end, I decided I would behave as I do with the kids of my close friends. If they were at my home, I would look after them, ask them how they were doing, but also not let them run riot – the Indian mum still lives in me – and generally be kind, loving and, well, not a dick.

On a family holiday to the Costa Brava a few years ago, we were sitting on the terrace of a restaurant for dinner, tourists buzzing around us still eating giant ice creams and sporting lobster-red shoulders from being stingy with the sunscreen. As we waited for dessert, we played a game we'd just made up. We've always done this as a family, and it can mean that long car journeys feel like minutes. This game, devised by Shabby, who is the soppiest of the family, was to go round the table saying one thing you loved about each person.

I'll never forget what Maiya said about me. 'What I love about Pri is I can ask her anything. It doesn't matter if it's difficult or personal, she always answers me honestly.'

What kids want more than anything else is consistency, because with it comes security. They need to know where they stand with the adults in their lives. That they aren't left confused by being treated with great love one day, then indifference the next. That the adults around them are open and honest. There is not much that we don't talk about as a family – in fact, I can't think of anything that is totally off limits.

When I saw Shabby casually handing Maiya tampons as she called out from the toilet, or explaining to Otis why grown-ups had pubes, I knew we'd never be the kind of parents all British Asians of our generation had grown up with – where the list of taboos was long enough to run into pages.

Shabby and Amanda, despite their differences, have always been united in treating their kids as people with their own viewpoints, not as things to mould into their idea of them. Two very relaxed parents who took their children to festivals like Glastonbury, while still living their lives of fun and pubs and partying post-kids. They've also spent a huge amount of time doing things with their children. Playing games, writing stories, drawing or going off on adventures free of electronic distractions. Giving them their time, more than anything. But they were mindful that relaxed parenting didn't equate to anarchy. Both Amanda and Shabby have always been very clear that they wanted to raise good human beings who cared about other people and treated those around them with kindness – learn to say the four magic words 'please', 'thank you' and 'sorry' – to bring them up to be people who had self-respect and self-worth but also cared about the world.

This was apparent in the fact that I've never heard Shabby badmouth Amanda in front of the kids, and by their accounts, she has never tried to poison them against him in any way. The result of this is that in over a decade of us being in each other's lives, Maiya and Otis have never once said anything remotely hurtful to me, and, hopefully, I haven't to them.

This is not a trivial achievement. I have heard of so

many families who experience teething pains when they combine households, sometimes causing resentments that start to bite in the years to come. The fact that we have all got on so well has been the result of each of us being loving and respectful to each other, and also because sometimes I step out of the way and let Shabby just enjoy being with his kids. And, in turn, when they now visit us (first in France, now in Spain), despite not seeing their daddy in a while, they'll always offer to baby-sit Leela so the two of us can go out and grab a drink. Time that we usually spend talking about just how bloody great our kids are.

~

When Leela began to start to ask about 'peach' and brown skin tones and to wonder about her own identity, I knew Maiya and Otis would be the perfect people to ask. They've grown up with a white British mum and a father of Bangladeshi origin, and I've been privy to a fair share of their race-related issues over the years through Shabby (like the time he threatened to out Otis's head-master to the press as a racist after he told Otis he couldn't dye his hair like his classmates had because 'it didn't match his skin tone'; or the tales of entitled ignorance Maiya experienced during her time at Durham univer-sity). The other day, I decided to have my own in-depth conversations about how they feel about their identity. Now at twenty-five and eighteen, Maiya and Otis have grown up to be thoughtful adults who I knew would be honest and open with me about this in a way we at their age couldn't imagine being with our elders.

'When I was six and Mummy was pregnant with Otis, I was hoping he would be white,' Maiya confessed.

'What?!' Otis was genuinely shocked by this revelation.

Maiya explained: 'It wasn't that I wanted Oaty to be white or because I thought there was anything wrong with me. But all we'd see on TV back then were little white kids, and they looked so wholesome, so this idea that white was the ideal and darker skin was less desirable, even ugly, was internalized.'

Both of them grew up with very little connection to their father's culture. Shabby has had a complicated relationship with his Bangladeshi upbringing, especially seeing as it is so intrinsically connected with Islam, something he rejected spectacularly the moment he left home for university and sparked up a joint.

'I just didn't want to be a hypocrite,' Shabby said, when I asked him about it. 'My culture or religion didn't define me, so why should I shove any of it down their throats? I didn't want to be like one of those Muslim guys who'd drink but wouldn't let their kids touch pork.'

Otis is of the opinion that his daddy needn't have been quite so dramatic.

'Whenever we talked about going to Bangladesh,' he reflected, 'Daddy never seemed that keen. He was always like, "We'll go to India first, there's more to do and see there." When I asked him why we can't speak Bengali, he said it was because he didn't want to be the guy that came home speaking in a weird different language.' Both Otis and Maiya are frequently frustrated whenever they visit Shabby's family and don't understand a word being spoken.

The problem with Shabby not raising his kids as part Asian is that for the longest while they didn't realize they were brown at all. Otis recalls the exact moment he was made aware he wasn't white. He was at a friend's house with a group of his mates when he was twelve, playing Nintendo Wii. To start the game, each of them made avatars representing themselves. Otis is probably the lightest-skinned of all of us, and sometimes gets confused for being Spanish or Portuguese. 'They made the skin of my avatar really dark and I was like, "Is *that* how you see me?"' It wasn't the shade of brown they chose for his skin that weirded him out, it was more an *Oh. People really see me differently.*

Both have experienced racism. Maiya has had strangers shouting 'Paki' or 'terrorist' at her but hasn't knowingly experienced it from anyone she knows, classmates, colleagues or bosses. Otis, meanwhile, revealed, 'I can just be walking down the street and people will spit on me or throw cans and stuff like that. At school, kids were making terrorist jokes about me, and the teacher said, "You can't make fun of the Pakistani." They couldn't even be bothered to find out I'm not Pakistani.'

A couple of years ago, he made an impassioned speech in support of Black Lives Matter on his YouTube channel, which led to local kids embarking on a hate campaign that saw their house periodically pelted with egg and Amanda's car vandalized. Rather than help, the police suggested Otis could stop the situation escalating by deleting his channel and referred to Amanda as his 'foster mum'.

Given their experiences, I wanted to know how and when they thought Shabby and I should talk to Leela about identity and racism. 'I think kids should just stay innocent and pure for as long as possible,' Maiya said. 'If Leela finds out people discriminate against brown people she might start to feel like there's something wrong with her, before understanding why. I remember when we learnt about Nelson Mandela and apartheid at school, everyone was looking at me as the only brown person. Kids deserve to live in their blissful little bubble. We don't have to be the ones to pop it.'

Maiya does believe representation is important and thinks it's great that schools in the UK celebrate other cultures and traditions beyond Christmas, but feels we need to tread carefully so that brown kids don't feel like they're too different from their white friends, especially if they live in predominantly white areas.

Shabby feels the same way and is reluctant to talk about racism to Leela just yet.

Otis and I feel differently. I remember so clearly the first time I was made to feel different and was taken aback by having no warning, and he agrees. 'I felt like it was super unfair that I didn't get that sort of information when I was growing up. It's such a big thing to have to work out and deal with when it happens.'

He added, 'I feel like it's better to explain racism to kids bit by bit rather than just keeping it away from them. Because it's not a perfect world and these things are always going to be there. So it's better to prepare them for that, rather than just keeping that part of life away, because it's something that we're all going to deal with at one point.'

Because it will happen. Show me anyone that's grown up in the West and claims to never once have experienced racism and I'll show you a white person.

~

One evening, a few months before I talk to Maiya and Otis about how they feel about their own identity, Leela is in the living room. Her thick black hair still damp from being washed, she is sitting on our squashy blue velvet sofa in Barcelona, the huge cushions almost swallowing her whole. It's been two years since Elsa-braid-gate and I have spoken to her about race and belonging, but still not much about racism. She is writing little notes in her looping cursive script, the letters scrunched up together like eager children pushing past each other in a queue for ice cream.

I read one of them surreptitiously. It says 'Notes of Love' on the front. Inside it proclaims: 'I love you, do you want to hang out with me?'

She sees me peeking and says shyly, 'They're for my friends at school.' She blushes deeply, her cheeks going a strawberry red.

At times like this, when I see that her intentions are so pure and she gives her heart so readily to all around her, it makes me cry.

Part of me doesn't want to discuss matters as weighty as race and belonging with this little doll living in her fairy tale world. I want to wait a little. To let her live in her dreamscapes for a moment longer.

But I know that's not possible. I couldn't bear it if, one day, someone says something to her that utterly blindsides her. A little verbal dagger flung carelessly, leaving her mute with distress and unable to respond, just as it did for me when I first encountered racism in England.

The thing about someone making a comment on your skin colour is that, for most kids, it will be the first time they're made to feel not just that *something* about them is undesirable – clothes or shoes, say – but that they *themselves* are wrong. Imagine feeling that helpless and realizing your parents, who are meant to protect you from the horrors of the world, didn't give you the right tools to deal with it. I'm aware that no matter how much I educate her on this issue, it won't act as a talisman against all nastiness. What it can do, though, is act as a little warning sign for what may come.

As Otis is fond of saying, 'Come at me, bruh.'

7. Choosing My Brand of Motherhood

Just before Leela was born, we were living in Brighton on the south-east coast of England. Home of mods, rockers and hippies, its liberal, accepting environment made it feel like home to me too the moment I stood on its pebbled beach. I have a memory of waddling along the seafront, eight months pregnant, sniffing in the delicious waft of fish and chips (holding my breath when I got to the bit where clubbers left the beach bars at dawn and used the pebbles as a urinal), thinking about what kind of mother I'd be.

Would I be one of the hippie, organic-cotton-wearing ones who pureed their own baby food? Would I be a 'mumfluencer' Instagram type who boasted about the number of bottles of wine in their recycling heap? Or would I be all work and go-go-go, leaving the kids with the babysitter?

Throughout my pregnancy, I would squeeze my eyes shut and try to picture myself as a mother. Leaning back against my giant C-shaped pregnancy pillow in our bedroom on top of a steep hill in the north of Brighton, I tried to conjure up scenarios in which I took my kid out to the park, or made them dinner or helped them with their homework. I tried to imagine myself as one of those TV advert mums who laugh indulgently and shake their head when their kids track mud on to the carpet. Nah, more likely I'd turn into Kali, the Indian goddess of death, threatening to chop their toes off. Truth be told, time travelling into the future has never been my forte. My brain goes utterly blank and offers up the equivalent of that old TV test card that used to be on when there were no programmes being broadcast.

In my twenties, I never remember hearing or reading much advice on preparing for motherhood. I'm not talking about practicalities like whether to breastfeed or formula-feed, how to swaddle a baby or what type of nappies to use. I mean preparing for the seismic shift that having a baby brings, leaving every molecule forever altered by the alchemy of becoming a mother.

Every time I picked up a magazine like *Cosmopolitan* or *Marie Claire* back then, they were full of quizzes to tell you what sort of girlfriend you were, how to figure out what sexual positions would feel good (the headlines winking 'for your pleasure, not just his!'), or what swimsuit to wear if you were pear- or apple-shaped. Any mention of babies was advice on how *not* to get pregnant.

'You'll be a geriatric mother,' my GP told me, using that delightfully outdated medical terminology for mothers over thirty-five. 'Assuming you're able to get pregnant easily.'

I looked at him, startled by the way he put it so casually. I had been chewing the inside of my mouth, a nervous tic I'd had since childhood which, if I wasn't mindful, could leave the inside of my mouth looking like a cheese grater had been at it.

'And if I don't?'

'Let's cross that bridge when we come to it,' he said, a bit more gently now. After a lifetime of trying not to have a baby, now my biggest concern was that it might take a long time to get pregnant, if I was able to at all.

As it happened, I had very little time to contemplate motherhood.

~

'How about we go and get some oysters and champagne at the Saturday market?'

A few weeks after I sweated my guts out in that Mayan sweat lodge in Tulum, swimming in the tropical sea at nearly midnight, I found myself in a very different weather zone – autumnal Geneva.

I was on a work trip, staying across the border of Switzerland in France with one of my dearest friends, Faith. A blonde, book-obsessed American, Faith is one of life's pleasure-seekers. She loves to travel more than anyone I know, paints, sings and writes, cooks and generally loves life. When she comes up with an idea of something fun to do – and especially when it involves champagne – I rarely say no.

But all week, I had been waking up extremely nauseous yet ravenously hungry, simultaneously wanting to mainline hunks of bread and cheese while also feeling a vivid shade of green around the gills. I put this down to the fact that we had each chugged copious amounts of French red wine every night after work. I looked out of Faith's kitchen window at Mont Blanc, which was starting to develop a snowy winter blanket. I knew my period was due so maybe that was why I was waking up with the appetite of a heavyweight powerlifter. I looked at my period tracker app – it was a week late. Suddenly it dawned on me that my hunger may have been more to do with potential pregnancy than my period. I had been gearing myself up for months of tracking my ovulation and jumping into bed with Shabby when it was 'a good day for it', and wasn't expecting this to happen so soon.

'Um, Faith, I don't know if booze and raw seafood is such a good idea today.'

In the quarter-century between my periods starting at age twelve until this point in time at thirty-seven, my womb had been as reliable as a Swiss clock. Until I knew whether or not I was pregnant, I needed to lay off the oysters. Although Faith excitedly suggested stopping in for a pregnancy test on the way to the farmers' market, I didn't want to take a test without Shabby being there. Instead, we made do with buying vats of *aligbot*, a French concoction of mashed potato, cheese and garlic that tastes heaven-sent. I bought a tub to take home to Shabby.

Sitting in Geneva airport late at night, I called him to tell him what had been going on, thinking we would excitedly talk about what this would mean. Instead, we had a fight about documents that he was looking for and couldn't find and thought I had moved (in our entire marriage we have only ever fought about two things – him not washing up and me being overzealous with the tidying). By now, sitting in the harshly lit airport terminal at ten o'clock at night, I was cranky as hell and desperate for food – later on I would recognize the gnawing feeling in my stomach as the visceral hunger that early pregnancy can bring.

In a fit of pique, I opened the tub of *alighot* I had been saving to take home. I sat there, exhausted and with dark circles under my eyes, spooning in hefty mouthfuls of the (now slightly congealed) cheesy mash, with well-dressed French people gazing on with concern and disdain in equal measure while I glowered back at them. When I got back to Brighton, I slunk into bed, grateful to be home, falling asleep with the tiniest flicker of a thought of whether or not I really had a baby inside of me.

The next morning, I woke up hugging Shabby, a rare occurrence because I like to sleep as if in a sensory deprivation tank, in total darkness and silence, with nothing touching me. Not the easiest experience to achieve when sharing a bed.

Shabby and I had only just got married, but because I had turned thirty-seven, we figured we wanted to get the ball rolling. As I had that trip to Mexico planned, we'd waited till after that so as not to compromise my margarita drinking, and agreed to start trying as soon as I got back.

I sat up in bed with the tea he'd brought me, in a mug the exact colour of the purple Quality Street chocolate, part of the kitchenware left over from my first marriage. Looking at the mug, I briefly thought about how we carry these fossils from previous existences into future lives, and that I had once sat in bed with that exact same mug with another man talking about very different dreams.

Was I pregnant? 'There's only one way to find out, I suppose,' I said, suddenly feeling as exhausted as if I'd run a marathon weighed down by sandbags.

I balanced the pregnancy test on the side of the bath, and paced between the bathroom and bedroom. Maybe a watched stick doesn't develop? Urging myself to do something else, I started folding laundry, immediately dropping a pile of clothes on the carpet when my phone timer went off.

A glance down at the test told me there were two blue lines. We were having a baby. We'd got the test that not only tells you whether you're pregnant but by how much; next to the blue lines was pink text: TWO TO FOUR WEEKS. Our little baby was already the size of a poppy seed.

~

Before I got pregnant, between divorce and illness, life had thrown too much at me for me to spend too much time contemplating what kind of mother I would be before I had a baby. The way a woman mothers is influenced by her own mother, of course, whether you knew them or not, whether the relationship was easy or fractious. Mothers define you and the way you mother your own kids. They write the blueprint for your parenting that lies dormant your whole life, until you have a child and find yourself replaying the same phrases and reactions. All parenting is like this to some extent. Either you replicate the way you were parented, or you move as far as possible in the other direction – whichever way you look at it, your childhood is the lodestone for your future parenting.

My mum was loving but firm. She had a take-no-prisoners approach, which working mothers who commute long distances often need to adopt, to everything from cleaning our rooms to doing our homework. We clashed loudly and often – my dad and younger sister, Poorna, would have to dive to escape the shrapnel from our world-war-level rows. Teenage hormones no doubt played a huge role but I suspect a lot of our fights stemmed from the fact that my mum had been brought up in the type of Indian household where you never question or speak back to your parents, and I was coming of age in the 1990s, era of the Spice Girls and girl power, opposing ideologies colliding like tectonic plates.

We lived in a three-bedroom semi at the end of a cul-de-sac in the depths of the Kent countryside, surrounded by hawthorn hedges and Thatcher-loving Tories on all sides. Our living room was a blend of statues of Indian gods and goddesses, mahogany cabinets full of trinkets from our parents' travels, and the faint smell of the sandalwood incense that my mum would light after her evening bath when she would do her prayers in front of a little shrine in their bedroom.

On Saturday mornings, while my (white) school friends were still dozing in bed at noon or watching telly in their dressing gowns, me and my sister morphed into mini cleaning ladies. 'Priyaaaaaaaa, Poornaaaaa. Come and help me, I'm not running a hotel here, you girls need to pull your weight,' Mum would bellow up to our bedrooms. My jobs were hoovering and cleaning the bathrooms; my sister's were dusting and cleaning the garden pond.

I still don't know how Poorna drew the short straw, but most weekends I would glance out of the top-floor window and see her scrawny little form standing in wellies, dredging up the algae that was clogging the filter, goth bands like Nine Inch Nails blasting on her Walkman, muttering under her breath.

'Muuummm, can't we skip cleaning the house just this once?' we would moan, taking it in turns as to who would take one for the team.

'So I'm supposed to work all week and then clean the house all weekend, so you two able-bodied teenagers can play Sonic the bloody Hedgehog, is that right? Spoilt, that's what you are.'

Now I have my own daughter, I know exactly how thankless being a mother can feel. It's why I make sure, even though she's young, Leela takes her plates and cups into the kitchen, folds her school uniform and places her dirty clothes into the laundry basket. It's important to me, just as it was to Mum, that every member of the family shares in the housework. It's not a chore, it's doing your bit for the team.

But teenage me would sigh, knowing Mum was only just warming up. 'When I was younger, we never spoke back to our parents! We did what we were told,' she would say.

'We don't live in medieval times any more,' I'd mutter

to myself, stomping back up the stairs, squeegee in hand. This would be said in the quietest of voices – I mean, I didn't have a death wish.

The expectations that many immigrant families have that their kids don't waste all their time watching TV or staying out till the early hours of the morning partying were frustrating. I reacted petulantly to the feeling that my freedom was being curtailed. In one cringeworthy, idiotic plan, I made my friend Jennie call home (this was way before mobile phones, so we stood in a freezing-cold red phone box festooned with adverts for 36DD ladies called Sandy).

We were in a manky old pub in Dartford that was serving us cheap Tia Maria and Cokes and wanted to stay out longer. Jennie was calling to tell Mum that I was okay but that I didn't realize how late it was because, get this: I LOOKED AT MY WATCH UPSIDE DOWN. What an extraordinary level of fuckwittery I was capable of as a teenager. To Mum's credit, she didn't scream down the phone asking whether I thought she was a moron to believe something so ridiculous.

In pushing back so hard against what I felt was too-strict parenting, I conveniently overlooked my parents' experiences growing up. Dad lost his own father as a teenager, which meant he and his three siblings were raised single-handedly by his mum, an extraordinary woman named Parvathi, after the wife of the Hindu god Shiva. My mum had lived an unusual, peripatetic life in Ethiopia and Ghana with her teacher parents. Neither of them had it in any way easy.

I grew up knowing the story of how my mother had been born with a hole in her heart. In the 1950s there was no way of fixing it and no prediction of how long she would live. At nineteen, she had a life-saving operation, the first of its kind, and when she married my father four years later, she knew she wanted to try for kids. She'd been told having a baby could threaten her heart, but she wanted one anyway. She had risked everything to have me. But teenagers being ego personified in so many ways, I never thought of that when I huffed my way up the stairs to my bedroom.

~

Sometimes, even if you're not sure what kind of parent you want to be, it can be easier to define what you don't want to be. I knew beyond doubt that I didn't want to lose myself in motherhood, swallowed up whole by a life of soft play and forgotten life plans. This fear didn't come from watching my mother, who remains fiercely independent and has had a career for most of my life, but from observing people I knew in India who transmogrified into Mothers. They gave up their jobs and sense of fashion to cut their hair into mum bobs and bookend their days with packing their kids' lunchboxes in the morning and making their husband dinner at night. Not all Indian mothers, it should be said. But I knew many whose existence seemed totally alien to me.

But then mothers I knew in England didn't seem all that different sometimes. Did they really subsume all their hopes and dreams to get in a froth about school uniforms or making costumes for World Book Day? Or, like the small talk at the school gates, were these obsessions a distraction from the bigger truths of parenting? That raising young children can feel like being swept up by a kind of *Wizard of Oz*-style tornado, depositing you in a place that definitely isn't Kansas any more. That in order to bring up our kids we make sacrifices at the altar of parenthood, which only in half-lucid three a.m. thoughts can we admit quietly to ourselves don't always feel entirely worth it.

There were other things I knew I was adamant I didn't want to be as a mother. I would never shout or scream at my kid or, god forbid, lay a hand on her. I would never want her to feel like she was a nuisance or that I didn't want her around. I wouldn't lie, hide the truth or deceive her. The adults in a child's life – parents, older family members, teachers and other guardians alike – rarely acknowledge how much children understand the truth of what's going on around them, and I was resolute that I would never insult her intelligence.

So what did I want to be? I vowed to treat her in a way I would want to be treated. To be honest about life as much as possible. To make her feel safe and secure. It often felt as if I were writing a story, building the characteristics of the mother I designed myself as, not entirely sure how it would all pan out.

It has always been important to be truthful with Leela. Not because I felt my parents were dishonest with me, but there were just so many things, important things, we never spoke about. We didn't discuss me going to India at eight and leaving my baby sister behind. We didn't talk about the teething pains of returning to England when I was sixteen and my sister eleven, living as a family of four again, or the difficulties me and my sister faced trying to integrate into our super-white school. But then this is how people parented in the seventies and eighties. It would be unfair to have expected my parents to be any different.

I have consciously tried to be straight up with Leela about everything, leaving out details that are inappropriate for a young kid. On the whole, I've found a way to truthfully share most things no matter how big or small. Whether it's giving her the context for a grumpy mood by explaining how a friend had upset me, or that I am about to go on my period (I think it's vital she understands how hormones affect her body so that she isn't made to feel like she's a 'crazy woman' for having PMS when the time comes), or telling her I had a husband once before her daddy and I got married.

These were never things I was ashamed of, but once Leela got to an age where she became interested in adult conversations, I knew they had to come from me before she heard it in passing from someone else. This, I felt, would destabilize her – not the idea that I had been married to someone else once but that her not knowing something important about her own mother might cause a minor shift in her sense of how well she felt she knew me.

I decided to talk to her about my previous marriage when we were brushing our teeth one night. We often do this at the same time, sharing a little night-time ritual that for me carries with it an endless array of lotions and potions. Depending on her mood, Leela will take my jade face roller and smooth out her already baby-soft skin.

'So, Leela, you know how I've had boyfriends before Daddy?'

'Yeah, Mama, I know,' she giggled, massaging her plump little cheek with the face roller.

'Well . . . I was actually married before.'

Her eyes widened 'To who?!' I told her my ex-husband's name. 'And where did you live?'

'We lived in New York,' I replied, still not sure of what she was making of this information.

'Mama, I can't believe it. I just can't believe it,' she said dramatically, holding her face between her hands, having long discarded the face roller.

'What, that I was married before?'

'No, that you lived in NEW YORK without me. New York looks so cool. I bet they have the best hot dogs.'

And that was it, no further questions. But she now knew a truth about my life and that felt important.

~

I rarely dealt in guilt before becoming a mother. I refused to buy into everything that society burdens women with – the guilt of not having the right body, the guilt of not doing enough for other people, the guilt of not being enough.

But motherhood . . . I couldn't escape the potency of maternal guilt. Most mothers become acquainted very early on with this idea. The feeling that, no matter how hard you try, no matter how much you juggle, somehow you will end up failing your child.

Maternal guilt can be a pernicious creature. Somehow, once you become a mother, your guilt can turn into a behemoth that unfurls its tentacles all around you, touching many other things beyond parenting. Guilt at not keeping on top of the laundry, exercising often or eating healthily enough. The pressure to be Super Mum who gets it right at all times.

Then there's the inkier shade of guilt that extends to other women – guilt that you had a baby, while there are mothers who have lost theirs either in the womb or out in the world. Mothers who struggled for years to conceive, weathering loss after loss like weary soldiers. Or women who never manage to conceive, yearning for the babies they could have had, which they feel might just be out in the stars, waiting to be born. This too is part of the bargain of being lucky enough to have become a mother; a necessary acknowledgement of women who either may never experience what you have or who have gone through pain you could never imagine.

When I stepped over the threshold into being a parent, I realized that notions of motherhood seem to be a construct that women – and society – devise to hang a neat facade around a brutally messy and complex interior. I've never met a mother who is exactly on the inside as she seems to be on the outside, myself included.

Becoming a mother seems to involve signing a contract of permanent cognitive dissonance. Wanting our kids to be musical, sporty and arty while bitching relentlessly about taking them to those extracurricular activities. Hating the pressure to make Halloween costumes or bake cakes, while also wanting to be effortlessly great at them. Or vice versa, knocking out tray bakes like we're TV show contestants while yearning to just slide a Colin the Caterpillar into our supermarket trollies instead.

Motherhood strips away several layers of skin and makes everything feel more raw, more visceral, the highs exquisite and the lows excruciating. But it can also make us swallow our true feelings, squash them down somewhere between layers of cellulite, tiger-stripe stretchmarks and the silky soft scar tissue of childbirth.

I remember a conversation with a colleague when Leela was about to turn two. I told her I was going to buy a cake because my baking was appalling at the best of times – 'No kid needs to be subjected to that,' I laughed. It wasn't just that. I was also desperately sleep-deprived, juggling enormous amounts of work and yearning for my family back in England like a lost limb. I was just about managing to make sure I had clean clothes to wear to work in the morning. The idea of baking and decorating a toddler's birthday cake seemed as unlikely to me as flying to the moon.

She looked at me and said, 'But your daughter would probably appreciate something homemade so much more, right?'

I felt like I'd been punched in the gut, my face turning flame-hot. Logically, I knew I was being foolish for being so upset by a perceived judgement on my motherhood, by someone I barely knew and who didn't have children herself. But my lizard brain imagined myself as a character in a martial arts movie firing daggers at her with speed. Shocked by the violence of my mental response, I consoled myself that I was just tired. I wouldn't actually want to throw a knife at her. In the end, I said nothing. I just let that maternal guilt eat me up inside.

~

But so many things shifted after having Leela. Up until then, I'd thought I had a good handle on my identity. I was liberal, a feminist, curious about the world, and wore my dual Indian and British heritage with pride even though it wasn't entirely without complication. I mean, I don't think there's any way to seamlessly fuse identities from two countries when one was the colonizer and the other the colonized.

Despite growing up straddling two cultures, by my thirties I felt I had made peace with the multitudes within me. I was British and Indian. I was married yet independent. A scientist but spiritual. These qualities no longer seemed to exist as a binary, as either/or. I could revel in being all at once. It was my choice. This is what I told myself pre-baby.

But then we tell ourselves stories all the time about our lives and who we are – some truer than others. Memories are recorded in our brain as narratives, and so stories are how we make sense of ourselves. You remember that time you went to the beach as a kid and you dropped your ice cream in the sand and the car broke down on the way home. These don't exist as individual snapshots but as a story. Our sense of self is essentially a collection of our memories threaded together. If you were to wake up tomorrow with no record of anything that had happened to you until that moment, you would literally not know who you were. But just as a story is told slightly differently depending on the person telling it, our memories are rarely set in stone. This means that if our memories can shift with a change in perspective, so can our sense of self.

And nothing changes perspective like bringing new life into the world. Four babies are born every second. That's 86,400 new humans with complex thoughts and emotions each being created from a single cell every day. Somehow, the big bang bringing about the universe into existence doesn't seem so conceptually radical. Women create life out of seemingly nothing every day.

Becoming an adult can shift the scales slightly, as the empathy gained through maturity helps you see that life is rarely black and white but mostly shades of grey, and you understand your parents a little more. Becoming a parent yourself is what triggers a more radical shift. This is not to suggest that having a child automatically confers wisdom and understanding, but that it takes you down a road through which it's impossible to travel unchanged. It imposes a metamorphosis on you that can, in the beginning at least, leave you feeling more bug than butterfly.

When I was pregnant, I had been told by everyone around me how radically life-changing the experience of having a baby would be. Well, duh, I thought, obviously bringing a person into the world is going to be unlike anything I've ever experienced. But what I had been warned about were the prosaic concerns of all parents. Sleep deprivation, constant piles of dirty washing, your sex life dwindling to a quick grope on a Friday night. Even though I had heard women talk about a loss of identity and not 'feeling the same ever again', I wasn't prepared for the transformation that childbirth wrought on my entire being.

So I wasn't expecting the reality check that comes with giving birth. When you have a child, especially when you're a mother, life holds up a mirror to your face and forces you to really examine who you are, who you have been and where you are headed. There is no looking away, no matter how much you may want to. It challenges you to reconcile with everything you have neatly tucked away in a box.

Motherhood doesn't just radically alter your sense of self. It forces you to look back at your life through an entirely new lens. Sends you time-travelling into your own childhood, seeing it anew. It's as if, until you yourself become a parent, you view your childhood through a kaleidoscope – colourful, distorted and a bit blurry. Then you move it away from your eyes and all of a sudden you see the full picture. All the nuances you missed because you could only really see things from your childish perspective.

And this is what I had been avoiding my whole life: looking too hard at my childhood. One in which I was sent to India to live with my grandparents, not once but twice, while my parents and sister stayed in England.

I had loved living in India, and I had a wonderful relationship with my parents. So I chose not to examine their decisions under a microscope because . . . well, what was the point of raking it all up? Except every now and then I would have a conversation that would shake the box a bit. Rattle it around and wake up memories that had long been dormant.

The very first day I moved into my halls of residence at university in London, there was a gentle knock on the door. I opened it to find a smiling blonde-haired girl in a red hoodie. 'Hi, I'm Vikki! Do you want a cup of tea? The only thing is I don't have any teaspoons.'

Moments later, we sat on the carpet of her room, backs against her bed, stirring the tea with a biro, exchanging stories of our lives.

'You went to live in India by yourself? Twice? That's weird. Why did that happen?'

I'd never talked about it at length with my parents and so didn't have a snappy answer. I also wasn't ready to dwell on it then and we moved on to more important things like discussing the cute boys spotted at the student union bar.

Whenever I did broach the topic with my parents, the response I got was that it was simply something that happened. It wasn't ideal but there had been no way around it. The fact of my having lived away from my parents as a four-month-old baby, and then later on again for almost five years in total, was absorbed neatly and matter-of-factly into the patchwork quilt of my life. Whenever questions about this part of my life bubbled up in my mind, I pressed them down, not wanting to pry too closely.

But there was no escaping it now. Because mother-hood is the great reveal.

Becoming a mother strips away every layer of artifice, every piece of scaffolding you have constructed around yourself to conceal your flaws or to bury events you've experienced years before. Now, all the truths I had collected about myself were suddenly thrown into shadow, so I had to examine them under a microscope to decide whether I was who I really thought I was.

8. When History Rhymes

In my very first class of my genetics undergraduate degree, we talked about nature versus nurture. Our professor told us how the reassortment of genes that happens in the womb when the sperm fuses with the egg – a sort of genetic pick-and-mix – can influence the people we become and the characteristics we have. But those inherited traits are tempered by our surroundings and our experiences. So while life deals you certain cards, you can to some extent control how you play that hand.

In my student union, I spoke to philosophy students who would think about these same issues but in different ways. Once they were past torturing friends about whether that beer really existed or was just a tasty figment of their imagination, they grappled with the concept of free will versus determinism. Determinism states that our actions are dictated by external factors, part of a chain of cause and effect, whereas with free will, we make choices untethered to any external constraints. For example, a determinist might argue that a violent person is destined to behave that way because their parents were violent towards them; whereas a free-will advocate would argue that, despite their upbringing, they have the choice not to be violent. I was firmly in the free-will category and felt that people who blamed their childhoods for their actions were abdicating themselves of responsibility. At least, I did until I had a child. Then all bets were off.

The psychotherapist Philippa Perry talks about how in parenthood we can slip into 'an emotional time warp and react to our past rather than to what's happening here in the present'. This can explain seemingly outsized reactions to our children's behaviour – a fury over a child dropping food or not putting their shoes on. In her book *The Book You Wish Your Parents Had Read*, Perry describes how we might insist on our kids doing everything by themselves if our own parents had been overly protective, or how we might get enraged with our child spilling a drink if we had been severely admonished for it as a child. These emotions are the inheritance of our childhood, the legacy of which is often only revealed when we ourselves have children.

These emotional through-lines linking each generation's parenting with the next make sense when you think about how the way you parent actually started before you gave birth, before pregnancy, back to when you were a kid. Each generation is connected to the next, and the next, through this ancestral umbilical cord. When my mother carried me in her womb, the egg that would make my daughter was already in me, inside my mother's body. No wonder family rifts are so hard to bear, when each of our lives is nested within that of our ancestors like miniature Russian dolls.

~

When I realized that I needed to step up my game in teaching Leela about her heritage, I was still grappling with how exactly to parent. Even though I had been a mother for about four years, to me parenting still felt like playing the same movie on loop. Like knowing the words that the actors are going to say before they've even said them, then wishing the dialogue was scripted better.

Motherhood had unlocked a new array of emotions – frustration, despair and anger would rear their heads disconcertingly often. I felt as vulnerable as if my entire top layer of skin had been stripped off, and could no longer watch violent TV programmes or hear about distressing stories without wanting to cover my ears and go into the foetal position. Having a child had somehow made me childlike myself in response to extreme sensation. It was utterly discombobulating to suddenly find I wasn't entirely in control of my thoughts and emotions.

Before I could figure out how to navigate the balancing act of teaching Leela about India and Bangladesh without weighing her down with an avalanche of cultural expectations, I decided that I needed to first understand how to be a more conscious parent. It often felt that much of my parenting was tapping out an ancient Morse code laid down in my own childhood. It's not that I felt I had zero control over it, but I got the feeling I was tangled up in the puppet-strings of my past.

Just as Perry describes, echoes of my own childhood manifested in my parenting. So many phrases direct from the Indian Parents' Handbook escaped my mouth even as I tried to swallow the words back down. 'Don't talk back to me!' 'Because I said so!' 'I am not going to say the same thing over and over.'

In the early fog of parenting a newborn, like most brand-new parents I veered wildly between operating on autopilot for things I now knew how to do well – warming up some milk, giving Leela a bath, and so on – and careering along like a drunk driver freaking out over the unknown bends in the road ahead.

When she started waking every hour, staying awake for thirty minutes, only allowing us to sleep in thirty-minute intervals, I thought I was literally losing my mind. Beyond trying to figure out how to get her to sleep, and how to ease teething, I didn't have time to focus on *how* I was parenting, as long as I was fixing problems as they came along. Early parenting often feels exclusively about caregiving rather than anything else.

Then Leela got to be a toddler and suddenly how I behaved in response to her mattered a great deal more. How I spoke to her, how I made her feel when she made a mistake, how I explained things to her, would all be absorbed by her rapidly developing brain and she would internalize it, the good and the bad. I wanted to parent consciously, to understand why something relatively small could propel me into a rage. To be able to discipline her (I still have a bit of the Indian mum in me, after all) without punishing her or making her feel inadequate. This is easier said than done. When you work long hours, are sleep-deprived and dealing with a toddler meltdown at the end of the day when you can barely stand, parenting consciously can be the last thing on your mind.

As my parenting so often seemed to be an echo of the past, I found myself becoming obsessed with the idea of being unsure if I was the same person I'd been before I had Leela, wondering whether I would ever return to 'normal' or whether this was it. Whether this post-baby me was just who I was.

In *A Life's Work*, Rachel Cusk talks about how, when her baby had a nap, she would furtively engage with elements of her former life as if she were seeing a secret lover. I can relate to that. Even after I returned to work after we moved to France when Leela was nearly a year old, the feeling of never quite being myself lingered.

I had heard motherhood described as one of the biggest adventures you can go on in life, unlocking a human experience unlike any other. But even that description seemed mundane. It felt considerably more immense. Like stepping through a portal to another universe, your fingers stroking stardust and moonlight, knowing you can never return to your old existence, no matter what happens.

~

When we moved to France, I started working at the World Health Organization in Geneva, living on the border of Switzerland and France. After a couple of years, when I moved to the communications department, I was in an office that was essentially a huge glass-walled box, so there was nothing obstructing my view of Mont Blanc.

Whenever I needed inspiration to write, I would mooch over to the coffee machine, gazing at the way the green-brown of the mountains ascended into white peaks. I was staring out of the window one autumn morning when my phone rang, and a colleague from another department was on the other end. Our mutual friend Nathan had fallen off his bike one night in Geneva and had suffered a brain injury.

For quite a while, as he was recovering, Nathan seemed to be himself yet not quite himself at the same time. An extremely intelligent scientist, he described coming to terms with his ordeal by studying himself, watching for signs as to how his memory was affected and whether or not he could still be effective in a job that required him to process huge amounts of complex information.

I asked him one question a few times over those months: *Do you feel like yourself?* And his honest answer was that he didn't quite know. Neurologists tested his memory but, as Nathan pointed out, measuring a change needs a baseline recording and none of us make a habit of noting down basic characteristics about ourselves in the possible event of injury. I became fixated with this idea of a random event shifting the tectonic plates of your self. How you could never really know whether that shift was permanent or not.

By the time we talked about this again over a vermouth in Barcelona, a couple of years later, he said, 'In the end, I stopped obsessing over whether or not I was measurably different or whether or not I was still me. I decided that whoever I am now *is* me.'

Nathan is one of my dearest friends and my questions were mostly out of concern for his well-being, but there was a part of me that was selfishly curious about how this shifting sense of self can affect your identity. When something – motherhood, in my case – has radically altered your physical being, can you really stay the same person? Can you ever change it?

In search of answers, I returned to Perry's book, which I had begun using as a parenting bible. Perry encourages you to examine moments in parenting when you explode in anger or frustration to see whether there is more to that reaction than meets the eye. This means thinking back to your childhood to remember how you may have been treated in similar situations.

Some people remember their childhoods in macro snapshots, like those View-Master toys of the 1980s on which you would click through a succession of images – Big Ben, Buckingham Palace, a double-decker bus, and *ta-daa*, you've just seen London. Others can remember the nuances of their memories, right down to swathes of conversation had on a particular summer road trip.

However rich your memories of growing up are, though, few things can make you confront the emotional minutiae of your childhood like having a child yourself.

As Perry describes it, when you become a parent yourself, childhood memories long buried are dredged up by your subconscious and brought front and centre. More than just memories – which might include details of who was standing where when your parents announced their divorce, or what posters you had on your bedroom wall – parenting delves into the recesses of your emotional back catalogue, so you remember exactly how you felt when your parents said they were splitting up.

When your child's behaviour makes you unreasonably rage-filled or upset (maybe they're clinging on to the swings for a few minutes too long or they don't listen when you ask them to put their shoes on for the umpteenth time), it might be that you have a young child who understandably has no concept of time, and would much rather be playing with their toys than putting their school uniform on.

But sometimes, Perry says, those flares of rage in parenting can trigger memories of how you were treated at that same age, memories fizzing deep below the surface. Therefore losing your temper at your kid for not listening could be because you didn't feel listened to at that age. Getting rattled when your child cries out of frustration could well be because you were ordered not to cry as a child. When we parent, we react to our deepest fears and our most intense wounds.

Sometimes, understanding *why* you have an outsized response to something can dissolve its potency. Perry offers insights into why children behave the way they do – that not responding when you call them is because they are so absorbed in their task they fail to hear you, or that not doing as they're repeatedly told is simply them being distracted with something that seems equally important to them. It's always better to temper your reaction with their reasoning in mind.

Over the following months, I put Perry's advice into action when it came to my parenting, but this didn't really extend to race. Beyond buying Leela books with Black and brown characters in, I was still unsure of how to talk to her about complex issues of identity. My own feelings about race and identity were so tangled up, it felt hard to unknot them sufficiently to parent Leela about it in a seamless thread.

She remains so blissfully innocent about the world, it feels challenging to even raise it. Even though I had mentally admonished my friend Caroline for not wanting to talk about race to her child, I do get it. I want to prepare Leela without making it a huge deal. But ignoring it only means I'm not alerting her to the tripwires that lie ahead.

~

A reminder of what children of colour can encounter comes when I meet my friend Sally for lunch one day. We were in a hipster brunch place in downtown Barcelona, and had just ordered vegan burgers that arrive in bright-pink-coloured beetroot buns. As we eat, Sally (who's white) tells me about how her twelve-year-old son Ochie, who is mixed race with Afro hair, has had one too many kids touch his hair without permission since they first arrived in Barcelona a few months previously. This is considered offensive to most in the Black community because putting your hands on someone's hair – someone else's body – without asking is not treating that person like a human being worthy of respect.

Ochie had had problems in primary school in London too, despite the city being so diverse. 'He had little dreadlocks and the kids called him "tarantula" so he cut them all off and had a high top and then they called him "Frankenstein" and it's just . . . gahhh!' Sally exhales in frustration.

Schools can be hotbeds of racism – and teachers and

school administrators behaving badly emboldens children to be racist to children of colour in the class. Charlotte had told me that, as well as her daughter wishing she had a different skin colour, her kids have been called things like 'chocolate face' at school. But, more recently, it took a far darker turn. One of her daughters was called a 'Paki' and was told to kill herself. Charlotte was understandably distraught, and she only found this out from the school as her daughter hadn't wanted to worry her.

This shows why it's so important to talk to our kids about race. Just as being heterosexual and cisgender is the societal norm that all gay, trans and non-binary people end up having to define or justify themselves against, being white is the neutral. The thing against which all races are 'other'. Whether I like it or not, my daughter, who turns the colour of dark chocolate in the summer, *will* be seen as 'other'. The older she gets, the harder it will be to protect her from that.

I only have to think about a moment a few months ago when we were in a taxi on the way to Barcelona airport. I was chatting to the driver in Spanish, who was asking where we were from (that question again). He ignored the fact that I said we were British, Indian and Bangladeshi and said there were a lot of Pakistani taxi drivers in Barcelona, and then pointed, 'Look, there's a whole row of Paki drivers there!' And then he just kept saying it. 'He's a Paki, there's another Paki. There are so many Pakis!' Now, I know that in Spain the P-word is used as a short form that is not really meant to be derogatory, just as Chinese-run bazaars are called 'Chinos' (the Spanish word for Chinese) for short. But I couldn't stay silent and I explained to the taxi driver that actually that word was offensive and has been used as a slur against anyone of South Indian descent. He didn't seem to get it, or maybe didn't want to get it, and insisted it was just a short form. We'd arrived at the airport so I gave up. Then Leela goes, 'Mama, what's a parky?' Oh, good god.

Barcelona is liberal and a welcoming place to live, but not the most diverse in terms of ethnic make-up. The only people of colour I tend to see are either taxi drivers, waiters or kitchen staff, corner-shop owners or selling tat on the seafront. It does make me conscious that Leela is growing up in a city where she won't see people with brown skin being doctors, teachers or business people. London would have that multiculturalism, but there are so many aspects of it that make it feel unliveable to me.

As Sally is raising her son alone (his dad passed away and none of his family are involved in their lives), she's 'hypervigilant' about what it means to be raising a Black boy in Europe. Before moving to Barcelona, she went on Google Street View 'to see what the racial makeup of the city was like'.

'I googled the Black Lives Matter marches to see how many faces of colour were there. I read every blog by every Black person travelling to Barcelona. But, ultimately, there's only so much research you can do.'

She brought Ochie over to Barcelona for a holiday to see what it felt like and, as he loved skateboarding and being by the sea, they moved. Although it hasn't been perfect, Sally sees how her son is starting to embrace his hair and love of bright colour and feels proud.

The question of where to raise your kids is different for parents raising brown or Black kids than it is for those raising white kids, as race adds another complex dimension. As well as wanting a safe neighbourhood and good schools and green spaces for them to run around in, there are also questions like how much racism will they face? Will they be the only brown or Black face? What will that mean for how they feel they belong? And the thing is, it's hard to prioritize multiculturalism at the expense of quality of life, which Barcelona has in spades.

Sally explains that when she was grappling with this issue, the main question in her head was should she close doors? 'Do I not open up experiences to him for fear of him being the only person of colour? Do I keep him near London where he'll see more people that look like him but his life experiences are very limited?'

This resonates with me so much and I feel like this will forever be a push-pull situation for us too, between wanting a life that suits us as a family even if it's not the most diverse. But there's always a nagging question at the back of my mind about what more I could – and should – be doing to engage Leela with her Indian and Bangladeshi heritage.

I would love to take Leela back to India one day – the trip we took when she was two years old was amazing but she remembers nothing of it – but it's not exactly cheap and easy to get there.

The day after Sally and I had brunch, I called my friend Sandi, who lives in a tiny village just outside Bristol. Sandi's family are from West Bengal, sharing the same language as my Bangladeshi husband, though not quite the same culture as his family are Muslim and hers are Hindu.

Sandi and I first met at Shabby's fortieth birthday party in Brighton. The party was debauched and huge fun. Sandi and I hit it off and soon Shabby and I met her boyfriend, Sam, who she's now married to, and we'd all go raving together. The last time we properly hung out, we both had day-glo face paint on from a club night we'd gone to the night before. Life couldn't be more different now, for both of us. Shortly after Shabby and I left Brighton, Sandi and Sam moved away too and now have three little kids running around. Both of them are hospital doctors and to say that life is intense is an understatement.

As she lives in a small, predominantly white, right-wing village, like the places Sandi and I both grew up in, I wanted to know how she felt about raising kids without much diversity around them.

As soon as we're speaking, her warm laugh spills out through my phone as she tells me about her home life. 'Mate, it's carnage. My youngest has just turned one and Viv [the oldest] has just started school. Sam works all the time, I've got insane on-call hours too and we don't live near enough my parents to see them much.'

Sandi's full name, Sananda, means 'joyful' in Sanskrit, an apt name for such a warm and lovely human being.

But when she was at school one of her teachers decided that name was too 'difficult' for her to say and shortened it to Sandi. That teacher had no right to do so, but teachers hold such authority when we are children that we often go along with it.

'I can't believe I let her do that, and really wish I hadn't,' she tells me.

Growing up in England with very few brown faces around, Sandi remembers that her family home and her parents were her only real connection with her Indian culture. 'Home was a little piece of India in this big white world I was growing up in,' she says. 'But the Indianness came more from my parents just being there. I don't know what to do with my own kids because growing up we did *Durga puja* [a Hindu ceremony to celebrate the goddess Durga] at home but not a lot else, and now, as Sam's white, I'm it – he looks to me to bring the Indian culture into our lives but I feel quite distant from it. Like, if I did a *puja* I don't really know what I'd be doing. And it would feel a bit forced, as I'm not even religiously Hindu – I'm an atheist.'

Sandi's voice gets softer. 'I'm really frightened of my kids losing their culture.'

9. Motherhood Means Death to Your Ego

I've always had a push-pull between parenting according to Indian cultural expectations and my own sense of how to raise a human – in a Venn diagram of my parenting, I suspect there would only be a sliver of overlap between the two.

Indian mothers traditionally give up everything for their children. The construct of 'Mother India' is a way of describing the country post-independence, using the mother as a metaphor to reflect a nurturing of society through self-sacrifice. My mum returned to work three months after I was born, being the sole earner at the time. For years, I had believed it was because she wanted to hold on to who she was, rejecting the stereotype of an Indian mum. But the more I spoke to her about it, the more it turned out that this too was a sacrifice, because, like any mother, she never really wanted to be away from her baby.

And sacrifice goes hand in hand with guilt – giving so much of yourself and giving up so much when you become a mother can feel untenable; and then when you're not giving everything of yourself, the guilt can be crushing. But unlike some mothers I knew, I wasn't willing to sacrifice my entire being for my baby.

Like many women of my generation, I was afraid

becoming a mother would mean losing my identity. This fear wasn't entirely unfounded. I had seen how when women around me became mothers, all the things that made them unique individuals – their love of sport, of fashion, of adventure – vanished, as if having a baby had caused these interesting edges to wear away, leaving only: MOTHER.

If I'm honest, I saw this in England just as much as I did in India. I've known women who were boxers and would pummel their opponent with relish only to hang up their gloves after having a baby. I observed women who loved to travel and see new places turn into anxious parents who either travelled with so much stuff that any journey became unbearable or they decided to stay within safe boundaries. I saw women who gave up ever styling their wardrobe or hair again, cutting their hair into a mum bob and buying their clothes at the supermarket.

Practicality certainly comes into it. The all-consuming nature of having a baby does subsume their mother's needs for a while. Not to mention that travelling with a baby can be beyond exhausting. But it almost felt to me like these women were saying that, those days are over now, relinquishing important parts of themselves as if it were a necessary bargain for having a child.

Maybe it was selfish and self-involved, but this terrified me. Did motherhood really make you lose your passions overnight? Goals you spent your whole life striving for exchanged for a tiny creature you would look after for decades to come?

Perhaps this affliction, this loss-of-self-itis, was because

I wasn't a young mother. If you have a baby in your late teens or early twenties, maybe being a mum is more an integral part of who you are. What I do know is that by the time I had Leela at nearly forty, I had spent decades becoming my own person, developing an acute sense of who I am, so having a baby was inevitably going to cause a dissonance in my sense of self.

When Leela was three months old, I travelled up to Edinburgh on a cold and wet winter's night just before Christmas. I had imagined feeling triumphant that I was 'still me'. That my intellect and experience as a science writer were still in demand even though I had just had a baby. That I would revel in nipping up to Scotland to give a talk, returning back to Brighton twenty-four hours later, the journey taking me from mother to writer to mother again.

Instead, after the talk I returned to my hotel room feeling like every molecule of my being was pulsing, in stasis, waiting to be reunited with my love, my little Leela. Because, of course, there is no possibility to transition from mother to anything, even for a millisecond. Once you're a mother, whether you lose your baby, whether they lose you, or some other horror in between, you are forever more a mother. No matter how much you achieve as a woman in your own right, no matter how non-maternal you may feel, your mother-ness is your baseline state.

I also fell headfirst into the trap of trying to do and be everything, both to myself and to others. In India, traditional ayurvedic wisdom says that a new mother rests for forty days after giving birth. She is fed special foods to nourish both her and her baby, and to help her body make breast milk. Mothers are encouraged to rest as much as they can, and not do anything strenuous, allowing the body to heal. When a prenatal yoga teacher mentioned this to me, I smiled and thought *No flipping way will I let myself be treated like a feeble creature. I am woman, hear me roar!*

How naive I was. My mum was willing to come and live with us for a few weeks as soon as Leela was born to make sure I didn't have to do too much. But I didn't want to feel helpless. This phrase 'having it all' – where does it come from? Is it something society forces on us? Or is it our ego in the driving seat?

Becoming a mother means death to your ego, the self that you hold up in your mind's eye. But in response to the inevitable loss of self that must come when you begin your servitude to the crinkly toothless creature you have birthed, it's hard not to continue to lead with our egos – whether that's 'getting your body back', killing it at your job or downing margaritas like the party girl you were pre-baby.

Journalist Rosamund Dean, who wrote a book called *Mindful Drinking*, describes how after having a baby she sometimes drank even more heavily on a night out with her friends than she would have done pre-baby. She wanted to show the world that she hadn't metamorphosed into a 'boring mum'. More importantly, that she was still her. In Dean's words: 'I might be a mum now, guys, but I'm still fun!' – the desperately cheery exclamation mark serving as the perfect representation of the discord between the aspiration and reality of motherhood.

The moment I had to let go of my ego was during breastfeeding. My milk supply was low, so I began weeks of seeing a breastfeeding consultant, of taking fenugreek tablets to increase my supply, of renting a double breast pump machine to crank up the old mammary glands. If you just flinched a little at how unsexy that image is, well, that's motherhood for you.

On the face of it, no one was pressuring me to keep breastfeeding; not the midwives, not my friends, nor my family. But the World Health Organization, where I worked, recommends that babies are exclusively breastfed for the first six months of their life. Society had drummed into me that 'breast is best'. But what's the corollary to that, then? Formula-fed is worst? How we feed babies has a lot more nuance to it than we allow women. We've somehow created a binary of breast vs bottle, when it's so much more complex than that.

It wasn't simply a sense of duty that kept me going. I felt like I couldn't give up on my baby, but actually what I was petrified about was giving up my ego. I'm not a type-A personality in the way it's generally perceived – someone who strides into a room making her presence known – but the desire to be high-achieving, to succeed (and feeling impatient when I don't), not to mention being stubborn as hell – that's me all over. So I decided I would not fail to breastfeed my baby because . . . I did not do failure.

Then came a moment of clarity that my ego couldn't argue with. I was sitting up early one morning in bed, both boobs squashed into the dual pumps of the machine, a bottle in each hand, feeling like a dairy cow. Still in the early stages of recovering from a C-section, this was brutal on my body. My scar hadn't yet healed and even walking around could be excruciating. The cherry on this particularly shitty cake was that my darling Leela, the absolute light of my life, did not sleep. During the worst nights, she woke up every hour.

So why on earth was I persisting with torturing my body into producing more milk when it just could not do it? It's taken me a long time to find clarity in the hallucinatory edge that early motherhood brought, but it was partly the idea that I could provide everything my baby needed; and also, as someone with an incredibly persistent character, I believed if I kept at it I would make it happen. But once that madness subsided, and we switched to part breastfeeding, part formula feeding, motherhood felt easier. My age and experience as a human being were life rafts that helped me tackle the new identity of a mother.

I don't use words like 'madness' lightly. In early motherhood, the border between sanity and the lack of it becomes so porous and blurred that we often drift between the two, some women staying in the sunken hollow long enough for it to become postnatal depression. Why some mothers tip into this state and others don't isn't an exact science. A history of depression or other illness can be a risk factor, but doctors believe that circumstance plays an enormous role. How much of a support system a mum has around her (one that doesn't disappear two weeks after the birth), and how many friends with babies she has nearby are key in shoring up women in the sometimes choppy waters of early motherhood.

I was lucky in having my husband around full-time; the magazine he edited folded unceremoniously, which – though stressful – turned out to be a godsend. We had savings that meant both of us being out of work was all right for a while, and Mum also visited regularly to help with childcare so that we could sleep, go out with friends or just take a bath in peace. My tribe of mum friends from antenatal classes all lived within minutes of each other and we would spend our days either at baby music classes run by eclectic characters (one we nicknamed Smokey McJaegerbomb as she always smelt like she'd just smoked a pack of twenty and was nursing a hangover – but we kept going as the babies adored her class) or hanging out by the beach, in the park or at one another's houses.

Even with all of this sanity-inducing support, I insisted on hosting a mum and baby cocktail party two weeks after Leela was born. I was still recovering from my emergency caesarean, yet I thought it made sense to produce a beautifully arranged table of champagne (served in crystal coupes), canapés and cupcakes. I had some scented candles burning as everyone walked into the house, complete with fresh flowers.

One of my antenatal-class friends, Sarah, and I talked

about it years later and laughed about how bonkers it was do this despite still having stitches and no sensation on the skin across my stomach. I think I was so intent on proving that I was still me, and that my love of hosting was undimmed, that it made perfect sense at the time.

I don't think it was only my ego making me do such things. Mothers seem to be more vulnerable than fathers to the drip-feed of expectations that seep in through our skin to convince us it's us who want to 'get our bodies back', have an amazing job, a great sex life, be stylish, have a fashionable and tidy home, at the same time as being the best mother ever, making our own organic baby food and brain-training our babies. Just writing that list was exhausting yet I have felt every one of those expectations hanging off me like a lead weight, and I know my friends have too. How we raised new-borns amidst this background noise of expectation is nothing short of miraculous. And when you're a mother of colour, the comparisons are tougher still as you are also measuring yourself – and are measured – against white mothers and the lives they live.

~

Lying beside a pool on a weekend in the countryside outside Barcelona, I talk to my friend Charo about the expectations she felt when she had her daughter, Adriana. A group of us have rented a house on the Costa Brava, surrounded on all sides by dense pine forests. The place is huge and has mini golf, swings and a climbing frame, just what we need to entertain the seven kids in our group, all under six years. Almost all the adults originate from other parts of the world – the USA, Germany, the UK – even though most have lived elsewhere before moving to Spain. Charo (a nickname for the evocatively Spanish 'Rosario') is a doctor who works for Doctors Without Borders and comes from southern Spain, still a fairly traditional part of the country, so I imagined the pressure was high and the tug of war between work and home life strong.

Lying on sunbeds next to each other under the hot summer sun, Charo and I gaze out over the pool at our gaggle of kids poking in the dust for insects together. She and her husband were living in Singapore at the time their daughter was born. Away from Spain, and from family and other friends who had kids, she felt no expectations. 'Most of my friends in Singapore didn't have kids so they thought I was doing an amazing job no matter what I did,' she admits.

Even if Charo had given birth in Spain, I wonder whether the intergenerational push and pull would have been as great as between my mother's upbringing and mine. My mother was born in a world where you only spoke when spoken to, where children did as they were told, where your parents were treated as gods who commanded every move you made. If this sounds dramatic, the 'parents as celestial beings' was a phrase my mum actually used to explain her relationship with her own parents.

In theory, I was having a baby in a more liberated time and country. Mothers in the West are thought of as having more freedom, being able to work, and generally 'having it all' compared with mothers in Asia and Africa. But if I'd had Leela in India, we would have had a cleaner coming every day, a cook, our clothes washed and ironed for us, and probably a chauffeur. Many women in India (those who are wealthy enough, it's important to point out) are able to work or create art or work for charities because the daily grind is taken care of.

Are mothers in the West really freer, or have we swapped one life of servitude for another? Most mothers I know, even when they work as much as or more than their partners, take on the lioness's share of housework and keep on top of the million pieces of life admin. Many mums, myself included at times, have felt like we're crumbling under the stress while our partners are doing less but still feeling like heroes. Maybe women in countries like India do have less freedom in some ways, but ultimately the patriarchy finds a way to oppress us no matter where we live. All that changes is the face that oppression takes on.

~

Motherhood forces you to park your ego at the door, while simultaneously holding on to your sense of self. The biggest thing I had to learn was that there is a middle ground between sacrificing myself at the altar of motherhood and never giving up an iota of myself for my baby.

Generations, both in the East and the West, are often divided about how to parent children. Older people, of my mum's generation for example, insist on parenting by instinct or asking other parents rather than reading endless books. I've had more than one parent with grown-up kids tell me that modern parents tend to fuss far too much over their children. They believe that worrying about imposing sleep-training schedules, fretting about what kids eat or interfering with their school education is classic modern-parent syndrome.

'In my day, children did what they were told. They ate what was put on their plate and, if they didn't, they went to bed hungry. There was no talking back, and they went to bed when I told them to.' An older friend reels out all the ways that parenting was stricter 'in her time', when I tell her about struggling to get Leela to sleep.

I didn't have much of a comeback, as I was still a new parent, but it didn't ring true to me that this way of parenting – where the parents were 'in charge' and ordered their kids about – resulted in healthy, happy kids. I've known too many of these former kids as adults who are either in therapy or really should be.

It's possible the pendulum has swung too far the other way, in some instances. I know parents who make their toddlers' healthy eating an obsession, spending precious hours in their kitchen at night (when they could be catching up on sleep) pureeing organic food that their children would then mostly splatter on the kitchen walls. I know parents who sacrifice their own relationship by sleeping in separate rooms (in one family, the mum began sharing a bed with her baby while the dad slept in another room; the kid is now six years old, and his parents have still never shared a bed since). This isn't to say that trying to give your kid healthy food or to co-sleep if that works for you is a bad thing. Just that modern parenting seems to be characterized by being utterly child-centric no matter the cost to their parents' sanity or comfort.

You could argue that this is the collective hysteria born of a 'snowflake' generation. But I'd venture that it's a natural societal response now that we know how the events of our childhood can echo well into adulthood. Many parents I know are also in therapy, unpicking the threads of their own upbringing and becoming conscious that how they parent will affect their kids.

With Leela, I decided to trust my instincts from the get-go. That doesn't mean I didn't talk to other new parents endlessly or read up on 'how to ease teething' or gentle sleep training, but whenever I came up against one of the Ten Commandments of modern parenting, such as co-sleeping is bad for the baby, or letting your baby 'cry it out' is the only realistic way to parent or you're 'making a rod for your own back if not', I trusted my own judgement and intuition far more than anything else.

10. The Baby Blues aka
When You Just Can't Cope

'Sending you to India just after you were born was the hardest thing I've ever done,' said Mum quietly when we finally got round to talking about the first few months of my life.

By now, Leela was six years old, and I felt ready to have a conversation with Mum about that time, so many decades ago, and why she sent me as a four-month-old baby to live with her parents on a farm in South India.

The first time we'd talked about it, the emotions were very different. It was Christmas, and we were all in Kent at my parents' place. Shabby, Leela and I had driven down from Brighton, and Poorna and her husband, Rob, had driven over from London.

Leela was four months old. The same age I was when I was sent to India. I can't remember how the conversation started exactly, but I was in my mum and dad's bedroom catching up, with no idea how far back we were about to go.

I was still on maternity leave, and Mum said something about me being lucky to have that time with Leela that she didn't have.

This was how that decision had been framed my whole life – as if there had been no choice. Hearing my mum describe it that way again, while I was holding my own gurgling baby, triggered something in me.

'I still don't understand why that was the only choice,' I snapped.

'We did what we thought was right,' Mum said sadly, sitting up in bed. 'Things weren't like they are now. We didn't have the choices you have.'

I looked down at my Leela on my lap and felt an explosive rush of rage – how could my mum have sent such a tiny thing thousands of miles away?

I refused to back down. 'I would have found a solution. I would have figured something out. Sending Leela away would be as incomprehensible to me as parting with a limb,' I fired back.

Mum looked visibly upset now, her head bowing lower, trying to hold back her sadness.

'It wasn't what I wanted,' she said. 'I just wanted you to be looked after.'

Now, when I remember that moment, I want to reach back in time and hug my mum tightly. To tell her she was, and always has been, a good mother. That she's always been there for me when I needed her. That I have never wanted for anything. That I am lucky to have her as my mum.

But back then there was so much hurt coursing through my own veins, not to mention the baby hormones, that I couldn't find any empathy. All I felt was distress.

Mum and I continued to rage at each other in tears, each of us time-travelling through emotions – she remembering her own sorrow at not being able to hold on to me, and me unable to comprehend willingly letting go of my baby and not having her in my arms for the next eighteen months.

Shabby and Dad tried to mediate, but there was no reason to be had.

'I can't talk about this any more,' I said, and stomped back down the stairs to the living room.

Rob looked up at me. 'You all right, sis?'

'Yeah. No. I don't know. That just . . . escalated.' I sighed heavily and sat down on the swirly floral sofa.

'Well, we can tick off the raging fight from our Christmas cliché list,' he grinned, which at least made me laugh.

It would take me several years before I could look back at the events of my first year of life with any understanding of what it must have been like for my parents.

Mum had me in another time far removed from the world of 2014 when I had Leela. In the 1970s, twenty-five wasn't a particularly young age to have a baby, but my mum had already lived a whole lifetime, having had heart surgery in her late teens. The ward she'd walked into for her operation was a cardiac ward filled with much older people and she didn't know whether she would make it through that brutal open-heart surgery alive.

Recounting this for my sister and me once, she described how in recovery in the hospital ward, she remembers waiting with the other heart patients for their evening meal. 'Pri, you will never believe what they served us for dinner.'

It was 1970, when British cuisine was at its nadir, so

my expectations were low, but we had to laugh at what she said.

'It was a whole lamb's heart on a plate.'

The idea of that as a meal being served to anyone makes me want to gag, but that they dished it up to people who had just had surgery on their heart sounds like a sort of sick joke.

Despite having been through so much, Mum had been highly sheltered as a teenager. In the traditional Indian family she grew up in, every decision was ultimately made for her by her father. When her family moved to England before she married Dad, she had a job, but all her earnings went to her parents.

When she had me shortly after getting married, Dad still hadn't found reliable work as a junior doctor and my mum was the sole earner. Mum then had to juggle looking after a tiny baby with an exhausting job where she would often be out of the house for twelve to fourteen hours a day. She couldn't cope. 'I had a breakdown pretty much every two weeks. I had to get a sick note from the doctor to take time off,' she revealed. 'I felt desperate.' Then my grandfather called her and suggested she send me over to them, and to my parents that felt like a lifeline.

I had a million questions. Hadn't they heard of babysitters? Couldn't she have found a different job with fewer hours? When I put all this to her, she looked down at the swirly carpet in the living room. Then pointed out, 'In the seventies you didn't have a lot of registered childminders like you do now, because so many women stayed home with their kids. There were all sorts of horror stories about nannies giving children medication to make them sleep. I couldn't do that to you.' As for why Mum couldn't change jobs, well, again in those days, good jobs weren't easy to come by. There was no possibility of working from home on a laptop like I can now.

It can be easy in retrospect to wonder why your parents didn't make different decisions, because the clarity of hindsight makes things seem so straightforward. I remind myself that parenthood – hell, even adulthood – is never straightforward or easy. Being responsible for a small human often feels like doing the best I can, while never quite sure I'm doing the exact right thing, at the exact right moment.

I don't know with certainty whether us moving away from England and our families, especially her brother and sister, was the right move as far as Leela was concerned. After we left France, the prospect of moving back to Brexit Britain seemed far less appealing than living an easy life by the sea in Spain. Leela may one day rail against us for living in a different country to the rest of her family. I don't know whether leaving her in the school she's in, which she loves but is not the most challenging, is preferable to bankrupting ourselves by putting her in private schooling.

All that Shabby and I can ever do is what we think is best, with the information available. To make choices that seem in our daughter's best interest.

And that's exactly what my mum and dad did.

'Your *Ajja* [grandfather] called me up and said that

since they had such a beautiful farm, fruit trees and animals, and lots of people to look after you . . . why didn't I send you there? And it sounded like it would be the absolute best thing for you.'

As a family, we have more or less made peace with the past and have accepted that the decisions were made with the best intentions. But it is not without complications. Even now, at forty-six, if you ask me whether I think I should have been sent to India by myself – first as a baby and again as an eight-year-old – I would say . . . no. Being separated from my immediate family so young has left an indelible imprint on who I am and how I deal with situations. I can sometimes appear cold and detached when things get painful in a relationship as a way of protecting myself; a sort of emotional parachute. For years, even as an adult, when I wasn't with the people I love, I would refuse to allow myself to miss them and would force myself to stop thinking about them. Now I can admit when I miss people but back then this was the coping mechanism I developed as an eight-year-old whose Mummy, Daddy and baby sister were suddenly, inexplicably, thousands of miles away. Human beings are incredible – no matter what we go through, our minds find a way to cope when our hearts cannot.

This isn't a criticism of my parents – I know they were making what they felt was the right decision. But the right decision can still turn out to be the wrong choice. For years, I pretended to myself that I was okay with that decision because it turned out all right in the end. Because, now, we are as close as ever. So why dredge up the past? The thing is, the past can be stirred up whether you want it to be or not – and nothing creates chaos in your memories like having your own child. Having a little girl now, it somehow feels important to honour my past self. The little girl I used to be, with thick plaits and big glasses and a huge heart who didn't know how to deal with what was happening, or why. It feels right that I acknowledge what that little me went through. That if I could go back in time, I would find a way to stay with my family.

What helps is trying to imagine myself in my mum's shoes. Struggling daily, hourly even, under extraordinary stress, with a tiny creature who didn't sleep. And then comes the offer of sending that little wriggly brown baby to sunshine and mangoes and an abundance of love. Isn't there the slightest chance I might have taken that option too? But whether or not I would have isn't the point. The point is that in 1976, as a twenty-five-year-old, my mum was making the decision she thought was best for the baby she loved more than anything. And that's all that matters.

But there was another thought that kept nagging at me. Ever since becoming a mother, I'd been thinking of the way my mum described that time, and something kept coming back to me: had she been going through postnatal depression? When I asked her this, she acknowledged that it could have been but that her doctor never picked up on it – it was not something people talked about.

More than forty years on, postnatal depression is still

a taboo topic. Like miscarriage and stillbirths, people hate to discuss instances when pregnancy and childbirth don't go 'right'. The times when parents aren't giddy with happiness. Of course, babies bring joy; but they can also unintentionally bring a lot of sorrow too. In the 1970s, postnatal depression was talked about even less. You had your baby, and you looked after it as best you could. What is clear is that, through no fault of her own, Mum simply couldn't cope, and didn't have the support she needed.

~

One in five women has depression or anxiety during or after pregnancy. This means that you are guaranteed to know someone who has been in the pit of a despair, wondering how they will claw their way out. The National Institute for Health Research suggests that women from ethnic minorities are more likely to suffer from postnatal depression, yet are less likely to seek help.

It's not hard to see why postnatal depression is still not given the attention it deserves. Especially among Black and brown women, living as we all do in a patriarchal society that's unwilling to care much about anything that affects women, from periods to childbirth to the menopause. It's likely also because of a connected and deep-rooted assumption that mothers are meant to sacrifice everything – their bodies, their sanity – for their children. The mother-as-a-martyr trope still plays out in our societal expectations of women, who are expected to stay home and look after the children, while men who do so are referred to as 'babysitters'. Even now, only 1.2 per cent of families with kids in the UK have a stay-at-home father. And this is in a country that supposedly champions gender equality.

Experiences of postnatal depression have started to be discussed a little more openly in society. But this has largely centred on the experiences of white women. As usual, when it comes to brown and Black women, we are at the back of the queue that leads only to a brick wall. If mothers of colour find it challenging to advocate for themselves during childbirth, when whatever you are experiencing is visible under bright day-glo lights, then trying to get the medical profession to take the nuanced emotions of postnatal depression seriously can be near impossible.

Candice Brathwaite was the first writer in the UK to draw attention to how Black women are discriminated against in healthcare in her book *I Am Not Your Baby Mother*; in the UK, Black women are four times more likely to die in childbirth than white women, and her own experience shows the series of inhumane missteps that make those statistics reality.

For British Asian women, the statistics are better but only slightly – in the UK, Asian women are still twice as likely to die in childbirth compared to white women. This is not because of a genetic predisposition or biological weakness; this is systemic racism at work. Mothers of colour are not listened to enough from the time they are pregnant to after they give birth. Brathwaite nearly died of postpartum sepsis after giving birth to her daughter, when doctors reassured her that nothing was wrong and she was being overly dramatic.

This is why I had a doula at birth. A doula is a trained birthing companion who supports not only you through your birth but also your partner. Crucially, doulas advocate for you during childbirth in a way that can be impossible for the person giving birth or even for their partner. It's not that I distrust doctors or hospitals, far from it – my dad and two of his siblings are doctors, not to mention many of my university friends. But I knew from speaking to one of my close friends that pushing for your own rights and asking to be taken seriously while in the throes of childbirth can be impossible, even when you have a partner with you – they are just as emotionally invested.

It took a while to bring Shabby round to this idea. He couldn't see why a doula was necessary and felt like it reflected a lack of trust in him and his ability to be my birthing partner. But as we always have from the moment we became a couple, we talked it over at length so we could see each other's point of view and he agreed because, as he said, it was my body going through this extraordinary process and if I wanted a doula to feel more comfortable going into the birth then he would absolutely support me.

I found my doula, Clare, through my prenatal yoga class and as soon as we spoke I knew I wanted her by my side in the hospital. It's a decision I'm ever grateful for. My labour was induced and the pain escalated quickly from bearable to agony. After a few minutes in a warm bath, I demanded an epidural. This is the moment I was most agitated about before going into labour. I had been told by so many mothers that they asked for one and were told to wait, and then were told it was too late. So many women made to endure pain that was so intense it was other-worldly, the kind that men would almost never experience in their lifetime – and if they did it would be an exception rather than the daily reality it is for many women. Clare spoke to the midwife and within minutes an epidural was organized. I will never know how quick it would have been without Clare as my doula, but I am grateful I never had to find out. Within an hour, I needed an emergency caesarean and was rushed off to the oper-ating theatre.

Shabby asked the doctors whether I would be okay, and they replied heart-stoppingly: 'We're doing every-thing we can.'

Those hours when I was being operated on were some of the longest of Shabby's life, and Clare was there with him, talking to him and stopping him freaking the hell out. He later told me that having a doula was the best decision we could have made.

~

Nature and our biology seem complicit in the idea of maternal sacrifice because it begins at the moment of conception. From the very second that ball of cells begins to replicate in our wombs, our bodies prioritize the baby. We may become dangerously anaemic, diabetic or malnourished while pregnant, in service of our off-spring. During birth, our bodies are pushed and ripped and scarred. Some of us never recover, and even those who do probably find their bodies never feel the same again.

A mother's devotion is not always an offering given willingly but a sacrifice wrenched by nature whether they like it or not. This might sound brutal. But then motherhood can be. No matter how cerebral we believe we are as humans, our bodies play out the ancient dance of evolution, in which one generation's primary function is to birth the next.

Although women are responsible for the survival of our species, we are expected to carry this burden quietly and uncomplainingly, and without enough emotional or mental health support for the extraordinary biological feat we have just performed. As a society, we've built cars that can drive themselves and found traces of water on Mars, but we are medieval when it comes to the business of having babies. After most major surgeries, people are put on bedrest and extensive medical leave, but by giving such short paternity leave allowances we force women to look after babies alone just days after their bodies have been traumatized; after my caesarean section, I could barely walk for weeks and lifting anything, including my baby, was a struggle. Despite the fact that suicide is the leading cause of death in new mothers, and suicide attempts have tripled in the USA over the past decade, largely in ethnic minorities, we still ignore mothers' mental health.

Maternal rage, possibly one of motherhood's greatest taboo topics, has started to be spoken about by British writers like Saima Mir. Mir describes it as a rage 'that makes you dig your nails into your fists in an attempt to stop the fury from entering your hands, because if you don't stop it now, it will turn to something shameful'.

Luckily, for me these moments have been few and far between, but I've definitely had them. Shame meant I have never told a single soul, not even my husband. The moment that sticks in my mind is one evening driving Leela back from nursery when she was eighteen months old. I was especially frustrated at work, and constantly sleep-deprived. On this car ride home, she started having a tantrum in the back seat, because she was hungry or thirsty or just tired. I sympathized, but I was driving her solo and I couldn't stop on the French highway, where cars beep and will dangerously overtake you if you drive even a mile below the speed limit. So I turned the radio on to distract her, but that made her wail even harder.

'Leela, stop crying!' I snapped. She bawled even harder, her cheeks turning hot pink. I flicked my eyes to the rear-view mirror. 'What is it, baby? What do you need?' A pointless question because, even though she was speaking a bit by then, she couldn't have articulated her upset. Her sobbing became screaming.

Then I started crying too. 'I can't do anything now, I'm driving, I can't stop here.'

I cried harder and harder, only just able to drive.

I turned the radio up even louder and she screamed even louder. So did I.

By the time I pulled into the driveway, we were both

roaring, a baby lion cub and her emotionally battered mama lioness. I walked up to the front door, handed the car keys to Shabby without a word so he could take her out of her car seat, and went to lie on my bed, utterly ashamed of my behaviour and wondering, not for the first time, whether I was cut out for motherhood.

Seven years later, when I reflect on this, I feel a rush of empathy for the past me. It was incredibly difficult working long days in a tough, full-time job and having a baby who hated sleep. Shabby was a godsend, who cooked every day, packing me delicious lunches, and was, and still is, a great father. But all my family were in another country, and I grew to truly hate living in France. I never understood the English Francophilia no matter how much I tried. In that part of the country especially, near the mountains, there was just one way of doing things and you either complied or you didn't. You mowed your lawn on Saturday, went for a walk or bike ride on Sunday, winter clothes came out on the first of October no matter how mild the weather, and so it went on. This reminded me too much of years spent in the tiny town of Mangalore in India, where things were done Because That's How We Do Them. It was not for me.

And so in those early days of Leela's life, there was little to soothe my soul. Which is why sometimes, when she screamed, I screamed too. I just wish I hadn't felt so alone in that feeling, that I had not been too ashamed to speak to other mum friends about it. Now I don't feel that shame any more. As author and academic Brené Brown has said, the antidote to shame is empathy. And for that new mama I was seven years ago in that car, I have nothing but empathy and love.

Even when I started working full-time after we moved to France, I was still breastfeeding Leela in the mornings and evenings. By now, she was eating solids and having formula milk, and so she wasn't relying on my body for sustenance, but I was unwilling to sever that unique bond that she could only have with me. I knew that once it was over, it was over. I would race through my work and drive home literally yearning to hold my baby with every part of my being.

Often, she would gurgle at the door when I got back, pressing her warm fat little body into mine. Sometimes, though, because she hadn't seen me for eleven hours and had been with Shabby all day, she would be disorientated at this sudden shift in the day and actually pull away from me and towards him. One evening when I arrived home and scooped Leela up into my arms, she burst into tears and tried to squirm away from me with all the force her tiny body could muster.

Those moments of rejection felt like a jagged heartbreak. I would run upstairs, my heart feeling like it was shattering into a million pieces, and then sob, shoulders heaving. It is a singular kind of pain to be shunned by the same human being who was once fused with your own body, a body that had to expand and adapt to carry this new life, a body that would suffer pain and damage in exchange for doing so.

I'm not suggesting that a woman's main purpose in life is having a baby. At this stage in our global population

(7.8 billion and counting), we could all let our baby-makers rest a while without fear of the species dying out. And it's obvious that life can have immense purpose and meaning without having anything to do with babies.

But what I *am* saying is this: once you've entered into that biological pact and had a child (planned or not), you hand over control of emotions, of your heart and soul, to another. You don't just fall in love with your babies, you are submerged. Which is why that mother-love sometimes feels so overwhelming, both for the baby and the mother.

When Leela pulled away from me at times, I would question why I was working full-time, why I hadn't chosen to stay at home with her instead – what job was really worth missing out on my baby's affection? Then, like a mantra, I would repeat all the reasons why we had made the leap into a new country where none of us spoke the language, until my heartbeat slowed and my tears dried.

I can't begin to imagine what it felt like for my mama. When she was finally able to travel to India to see me for my first birthday (they could only afford for one of them to travel, so she flew alone), it had been eight months since I had seen her. She didn't want to overwhelm me by picking me up immediately, especially as my grand-father warned that I hated going to anyone but my grandmother, so she waited until I seemed comfortable being around her; how she had the willpower not to cuddle me as soon as she saw me, even though she must have been dreaming of that reunion, proves to me how she has always put my needs first.

Reflecting on my own experiences of birth and those of my mama, I still had questions. I have the most loving parents in the world, so despite all the issues with childcare and potential postnatal depression, how could they have made the decision to send me away? And nearly forty years after I'd had my 'oh wait, I'm actually brown' realization in that freezing cold playground in England, it gutted me that my daughter was having the same thoughts herself. Feeling like a shapeshifter, neither one thing nor the other.

If this were a movie, there would be some seriously emotional music dialling up right about now. How was this possible, that in four decades we have made such little progress in race that my kid was struggling with the same identity issues that I had grappled with?

All of a sudden, with a giant swoosh of love and understanding, I got it. I finally understood why my parents had so wanted me to experience being in the undulating brown ocean of 1.2 billion people that is India.

Where you, as a brown person, are in the majority for once. Where, if kids had been playing a game of 'which ice cream would you be', the only answer would be a resounding: CHOCOLATE!

11. A Brown Bloke and a *Bébé*

'I had mostly been a weekend dad until Leela came along, and I had it easy – you do fun stuff, buy them doughnuts, take them to fun fairs, and they love it,' says my husband, Shabby. 'But I needed to prove to myself that I could do the day-to-day grind of parenting just as well.'

After we moved to France when Leela was eleven months old, I had to go back to full-time work. As Shabby wasn't working, he was by default the one who would stay at home with Leela, but he actually wanted to be a stay-at-home father.

In our little French village of Ségny, where many mums don't work (or if they do, it's often part-time), a British-Bangladeshi stay-at-home dad was like a unicorn. I had a constant stream of people telling me how lucky I was to find a man who was happy to change nappies and make baby food all day long. Not unsurprisingly, this raised my hackles. Where was my praise and adulation for hustling at work all day long in a job that was so stressful my hair was starting to fall out? Praising men for doing even the most basic acts of childcare or housework is still incredibly common.

But I decided that resentment – either for the praise or for the time he was spending with our baby – was not constructive. It would eat away at me and our marriage, and it wasn't Shabby's fault that society had such a low bar for what being a good father meant. So I thought about the positives. In much the same way that men with kids can achieve what they do because of their wives staying at home or working but carrying the family load, one reason I have the career I have today is because Shabby stayed home so I could fly off to conferences around the world at a moment's notice or work late without thinking about what time it was. In the end, that career move to France gave us financial freedom (we were able to buy a house back in England as an investment and Shabby could retrain as a graphic designer), and the professional contacts to move to Barcelona to fulfil our dream of living in Spain.

I suspect that many women secretly (or maybe not so secretly) believe that they would make the best primary caregiver for their child. It's not surprising really. Most of us have internalized the idea that mothers should be mainly responsible for childcare, and society conspires (through continuing to make it hard for women to raise kids and have a career) to make that theory a reality.

However, the evidence shows that the quality of care matters far more than who is providing it – whether it's the mother, father, a grandparent or a nursery – and that parental contentment tends to outweigh anything else. Basically, if the parents are happy with the arrangement and their kids' needs are met, and they are engaged through reading and educational play and not just left to their own devices or plonked in front of the TV for eight hours, that's more important for everyone's well-being than anything else. Given this, and our circumstances, it made sense for my husband to look after our baby while I went off to work.

For our family, this was the best decision. We could have put Leela in a full-time nursery while Shabby worked, but neither of us wanted that, and he was happy to stay home. In retrospect I can see how important it was for Leela to see her dad be the main caregiver for a while.

If this is rare in British families, it's even rarer in ethnic minority British families. In South Asian families, toxic masculinity can mean that women are treated badly, forced to marry men they don't want to, and are denied careers. Here's an example. When we visit relatives in India, we always sit down to a huge feast – rice, dosas, various meat or fish curries and endless side dishes – as do many South Asians heading back to the motherland. A friend of mine told me about her elderly aunt who, at nearly eighty, is still at her husband's beck and call. At one family meal, my friend's uncle (the aunt's husband) wanted more rice. The rice pot was right next to him, but he made his wife get up from the other side of the table, walk over to him and serve him more rice. I was stunned, grateful that I come from a more liberal, egalitarian family where my parents share roles (my mum cooks, my dad cleans the kitchen; she weeds and plants in the garden and he cuts the hedge).

These patriarchal attitudes can be common across Asia, but machismo isn't just detrimental to women – when toxic masculinity is turned inwards it harms men too, and can stop men from seeking healthcare for both physical and mental ailments. Although this can be viewed as being related to how boys and men are socialized, there is a race element to it. A 2004 study of Pakistani immigrants to the UK showed how middle-aged Pakistani men had significantly higher rates of depression and anxiety compared with white British counterparts.

This makes it even more striking for my husband, born and raised to the start of his teen years in Bangladesh, to be a stay-at-home dad. This might be because our social evolution can be rapid. In the split of collectivism vs individualism between Indian and British cultures, studies show that people can switch the way they think pretty rapidly when their environment changes. In 2016, a researcher at the University of Exeter showed that first-generation British Bangladeshis who had moved to the UK from Bangladesh after the age of fourteen retained their collectivist attitudes even after many decades of living in the UK compared with second-generation Bangladeshis who were more individualistic. The researchers suggest this is the case due to the fact that much of our psychological wiring happens before the age of fourteen.

Maybe this isn't that surprising – that people born and raised in a different country to their parents would take on the characteristics of their new homeland – but it shows how important environment can be compared with inherited ways of thinking. It suggests that even second-generation Bangladeshis who observe religious practices and are in line with family and community expectations are inherently wired differently.

This makes me hopeful for many reasons. It takes

some of the pressure off me as a mother as I can see that, no matter how I parent, there will be so many variables that influence the person Leela becomes. But it also signals the possibility for change. It means that although Leela may encounter the same microaggressions I have done, she may respond differently. My generation can still find it difficult to respond appropriately for fear of being too aggressive or making others uncomfortable. We might stay silent when someone white says they hope to come back from holiday with a tan as deep as ours, or when a colleague waves their hand in front of their face at the smell of spices in an office lunchbox. But I hope Leela's generation will own their heritage more keenly.

Author Candice Brathwaite has talked about being raised by her grandfather and how it showed her what a 'real man' was: one who wants to look after his family and be present in the nitty-gritty day-to-day of parenting, who wants to support his partner in her dreams as well as pursue his own. That is the type of man she ended up marrying. As society will try to put all sorts of expectations on my little brown girl about what kind of job she can have and how she shouldn't leave it too late to be a mother and how, when she is a mother, she should be at home with her kids . . . well, I want her to know what sort of partner she should aim for.

~

Brathwaite is in the minority, however, because for most of us our fathers or other male relatives were always at work or elsewhere, and so what role models can we look to for how men should contribute at home? Even in 2021, men spend a vanishingly small amount of time on housework. In India, men spend no more than 19 minutes a day on household tasks, but even in the UK men are only spending an hour or so on chores while women in the UK spend 3.5 hours.

Societal expectations of men as breadwinners and women as nurturers clearly play into family decisions about who goes out to work and who stays home with the kids. When we spoke about this recently, Shabby said himself that one of the things that made the decision easy was the fact that, in France, as he didn't speak the language, finding a job would have been tough.

'In Brighton, I don't know that I would have been as comfortable staying home. I might have felt like I was scrounging off you. There's still something shameful about a man who doesn't work.'

But there is another reason why the number of fathers staying home has fallen again since the millennium. If you look at a graph of economic growth, in the year 2000 GDP growth was about 3 per cent. This slowly started falling until it plummeted during the financial crash in 2008. Although the economy recovered to a certain extent, it never rose above the growth of the early millennium, and the Brexit vote to leave the EU in 2016 caused it to start falling again. And we know all too well what happened in 2020 to cause the economy to sink still further.

The miserable truth is that in 2023 men are still paid so much more than women that they can't afford to stay home even if they want to. In addition, high childcare costs mean that women often save just pennies after they've worked all week and paid childcare, so end up staying home with their kids. Men are often paid 20 per cent more than women, and in some companies this pay gap can be as wide as 60 per cent. This clearly needs to change, because having fathers share in childcare as much as mothers will have so many societal knock-on effects, from empowering women and allowing them more freedom in their lives as parents, to providing important role models for their children.

Even in the UK, Shabby's role would have been noteworthy. The number of stay-at-home dads is extraordinarily small. But this is in contrast to a rise in stay-at-home fathers at the start of the millennium when numbers were beginning to go up. Some psychologists think this was due to a shift in societal thinking about 'new men', a novelty that started to wear off.

If I didn't have a template for being a stepmother, my husband definitely didn't for being a stay-at-home dad. Brown and Black fathers who stay home to look after their children are a rare species. And even those who do stay home are probably viewed very differently from their white counterparts. With no guidebook, Shabby had to figure out how to be a stay-at-home father through trial and error.

In France, we had a terrible internet connection, which meant that even the little bit of TV time he would have given Leela was out. 'At first, I would do everything I knew to entertain her, drawing, singing, running around the garden. Then I'd look at the clock and it was only ten a.m.' As Leela slept a lot during the day, Shabby started experimenting with cooking and trialling new recipes. Even when she was awake, 'Leela was happy just playing with something on the kitchen floor, watching me chop onions, and so we got into a great rhythm.'

It's clear to me that this bonding period meant that Leela got the best of us. She has Shabby's endless patience and his love of drawing and art. She has my love of science and curiosity about the world, and my obsession with travel. And I'm convinced that this deep connection with both of us has led to Leela being an extremely secure human being. While I don't tend to go in for parenting theories all that much, attachment theory posits that a secure child trusts other people easily, is in tune with their emotions and can communicate when they are upset. This is Leela down to the ground.

~

Shabby and I were packed into a French school hall one December night, waiting for our three-year-old daughter's first school production. All week she'd come home from her preschool humming French songs to herself, and I couldn't wait to see my curly-haired cherub perform on stage for the first time ever.

As her classmates started to file out on to the stage, my heart suddenly skipped a nervous beat. The kids were all dressed in either feathered headdresses or some approximation of John Wayne. I knew that the same thought had flown like a startled bird through my husband's head too: they were going to be 'cowboys' and 'Indians'.

Please let Leela not be a Native American, I thought.

In the end she was a 'cowboy' but I don't know if that was worse. They sang songs and the 'cowboys' circled the 'Indians', who even used the hand-over-mouth gesture, generally used by white people in mockery of the Native American war cry.

This felt unbearable. This was the ignorant behaviour I had experienced in the early 1980s at school; I couldn't fathom this still being a thing in France in 2018. I looked over at another British mum, a few seats down. Both of our eyes widened slightly in shock that this was actually happening.

'Well, that was interesting,' I said to her when the show was over and we were all shuffling out of the hall, bewildered at the bizarreness of the situation and the fact that none of the French parents seemed to think it was anything out of the ordinary. 'Do you think we should say something to the teachers?'

She sighed. 'I've already had chats with the head teacher about this. They genuinely don't think there's anything wrong with it and insist they are just sharing other cultures.'

On the way home, I wondered whether I had the energy to try and raise it with the school. And if I did, would it make a difference? It might seem obvious that I should have tried to do something, to make some change happen. But when you differ from the norm – whether that's being LGBTQIA+, fat, disabled, or a person of colour in a mainly white country – there are so many microaggressions that you can encounter on a daily basis. You have to make constant judgement calls about whether you have the energy to engage in what will at best be a heated conversation or, at worst, a fight about it. I don't always have the energy, and that day was one of those times I just had to let it go.

I seemed to be constantly tired in those days. When we moved to France, Leela was not even a year old. She was babbling a bit but not yet walking – she took her first steps in the kitchen of our French rental house as we were unpacking boxes, with the Beastie Boys blaring out of the radio.

A year in, motherhood felt simultaneously easier and colossally harder than the newborn days. We moved at the start of July. But six weeks previously, Rob had taken his own life after years of suffering from depression and being a heroin addict, leaving my sister agonizingly distraught and our family in mourning.

Leela had always been a poor sleeper at night and the move to France threw any sort of progress we'd made with her sleep out of the window. We woke up with Leela what felt like a thousand times a night, meaning that morning brought red, scratchy eyes, and felt barely any different from being asleep. I had Zoom calls with a therapist while at work, and would often do those calls in my car, air con cranked up high to fend off the heatwave France was having. Once, after an especially heavy session that left me sobbing, I saw repeated messages and emails from my boss asking why I wasn't answering my phone. It was my lunchbreak, but there was no respite from the endless workload.

Those days made me feel about as unmoored as a

mother as I have ever felt. If I couldn't get it together for myself, how on earth would I provide support for a baby?

Bringing up a brown baby in France seemed to be another curveball I wasn't quite prepared for. We lived in a semi-rural wilderness on the border with Switzerland, and there was little around us except for a boulangerie, a pharmacy and a pet shop, plus a giant Carrefour opposite our house.

Shabby punctuated his days looking after Leela with trips to the supermarket, often twice a day just for something to do. Despite seeing him do family-sized shops so often, the security guard would stop him to check his bags, and Shabby noticed that Muslim women wearing hijabs or burkas were stopped too. Not a single white person attempted to intervene during these repeated, obviously racially motivated, checks.

I had the same issue in the Sephora near us. As I was working for the UN, I was dressed smarter than I ever had before, or ever will again, often in a sharp suit and heels. As soon as I walked into the shop, the security guard would start tailing me, sometimes so close to me that if my French was good enough I would have turned to him and said, 'What, are we dating?' People of colour are so often gaslit about these microaggressions, I tested this out several times to be sure. I would wait and watch a stream of white women walk through the door and he never budged. I walk in, and he pops up like a jack-in-the-box, never leaving my side until I paid. I thought about complaining but never did in the end. I knew I would get the usual response of it's just him doing his job, and my French was not good enough for an argument.

Whether or not France is more racist than other Western countries is a matter of debate, but it has made moves to discriminate against minority religions and races, controversially trying to ban women from wearing the hijab, the headscarf that some Muslim women wear. When we lived there, it never rang true that this ban was to stop women from being oppressed (if that were true, they would stop Catholic nuns from wearing habits), but rather to ensure that Muslims never feel truly at home in France.

The hypocrisy of only banning Muslim head coverings (hoodies and hats are apparently fine) is exceptionally galling given the recent French *Vogue* social media post saying, 'Yes to the headscarf!' alongside a photo of American actress Julia Fox turning up at Paris Men's Fashion Week wearing a black headscarf tied Grace Kelly style, as if she was about to get into a convertible.

France's approach – that immigrants should assimilate into French culture – can have some benefits, as everyone is entitled to the same rights and healthcare as citizens. But a 2016 national report on the state of racism in France reported that 34 per cent of the French population view Islam negatively and 41 per cent thought Jews were obsessed with money. Remember, these outdated views were being expressed just a few years ago. Despite so many people having clear views about people from difference races, around 33 per cent said they were colour-blind when it came to race. This perfectly sums up the challenges of dealing with racism – when so many in society express racist views, which means by definition that they are aware of race, but many also say they don't see race. Both can't be true at the same time. As Reni Eddo-Lodge and others have pointed out, this claim to not see race is singularly unhelpful in addressing societal issues faced by non-white people. Because when you don't acknowledge race, how do you talk about racism?

This, overwhelmingly, was the biggest challenge we faced in France. The refusal to talk about what was really happening.

Now that we live in Spain, the papering over the cracks continues as Spain point-blank refuses to acknowledge its Muslim influence despite Moorish rule lasting 800 years. The only admission you see is in the Spanish obsession with pork. Muslims don't eat any pig products, and so in a gesture of political and religious resistance or, to put it more crudely, a way to tell their former colonizers to fuck off and not come back, the Spanish have embraced pork in every meal of the day. It dominates the menu in every restaurant from croquetas to slow-cooked pork shoulder to slices of salami and chorizo. I've often picked up a menu to order and seen that pork features in three out of four main dishes. Now that Leela is increasingly Spanish, it's no coincidence that when she comes over to my parents' house in Kent, the first thing she asks my mum is whether she has remembered to stock the fridge with mini sausages.

When I went to Marrakech to write this book at the start of 2022, Charo, who is from Seville, came to join me for a few days at the end of the trip. Seville is in the southern tip of Spain, just the other side of the Strait of Gibraltar from Morocco, but Charo had never been before. Even though Morocco is only a couple of hundred miles away from southern Spain, it just wasn't a place people thought of travelling to, she says.

Even though Andalusia is replete with Moorish architecture, such as the Mezquita in Córdoba or the Alcázar in Seville, these are preserved for tourist revenue, and there is not much discussion of race or ethnicity in Spanish culture. You're either Spanish or you're not.

Yet the conversation about race, right from when children are very young, is urgent. Research from Yale University shows that in the USA, teachers' implicit bias against Black children starts as young as preschool. Imagine that. A Black kid as young as three or four, only just out of nappies, walks into a class, and their teacher is already likely to think they'll be trouble.

What is really telling is that the study went on to show that while Black children were more likely than white kids to be marked down for subjective behaviours such as 'insubordination', 'defiance' and 'disrespect', both white and Black children were equally disciplined for objective actions such as possessing alcohol or drugs on campus. Which means that the greater disciplining of Black children is due to racism. And these biases are repeated time and again in media and culture, reinforcing these stereotypes of Black boys being disruptive and Black girls being angry.

To me, it seems blindingly obvious that racism is at work here. But it can be the work of a lifetime trying to convince people who believe we live in a post-racial world or that most people aren't racist. And it's doubly hard to counter these myths when the UK government produces reports as it did in March 2021 declaring that 'Britain is not racist'.

Even when a person of colour grows their wealth, and is able to pass on financial and educational advantages, systemic racism still drags them down. A joint study by researchers at Stanford and Harvard universities shows that even when Black American boys live in similar neighbourhoods, go to similar schools, and are raised in similarly wealthy households, they still consistently go on to earn less as adults than white American boys.

These are not comfortable conversations to have with our children and with people around us, that's for sure. But while we have guidance on how to bring up girls not to have issues with their body, and to understand that they are equal to boys, we also need to guide them on fundamental issues of race and identity.

And this is especially important for brown and Black kids – even if you don't think of yourself as different, you can bet that, early on, others will start making you aware of this. Raising children of colour requires a delicate balancing act: acknowledging a world that is frequently against them while empowering them to live their lives freely without putting too much pressure on them.

12. Homegrown Racists

Though the British school curriculum skirts over the worst of colonialism in a way that shields most white British people from the full horrors, growing up in India, the reminders of English dominion were everywhere.

Given India's history of being dominated by a country that brutalized half the world, you might think that Indians would understand how to treat other cultures. But the most openly racist conversations I've ever heard have been in India, with dark-skinned people being referred to as 'ugly as crows', Africans being called 'monkeys' and Far Eastern Asians eliciting 'ching chong' impersonations.

When I had a Black British boyfriend at university, a Muslim friend of my mother's asked me if it wasn't disgusting to kiss 'those huge lips'. I walked away in silence, but as with almost all instances of casual racism, spent many hours later wishing I'd had the courage to challenge her abhorrent prejudice, one she didn't seem remotely embarrassed about.

This viciousness not only hurts darker-skinned people living in India, it causes Indians themselves to carry self-hating seeds within them that can grow and twist around their hearts, making them think that in a predominantly white country, they are inherently lacking.

But none of that should come as a surprise in a country that invented the caste system, designed to press one foot firmly on the necks of the disadvantaged, ensuring the elite and the intellectuals stayed at the top.

India's caste system began with the invasion of the Aryans, fair-skinned people from Persia and thereabouts, around 1500 BC. They created four main categories: Brahmins (priests), Kshatriyas (warriors), Vaishyas (farmers) and the Shudras (the so-called 'untouchables', or as this community prefer to be known, Dalits). Dalits were supposed to serve everyone else and were essentially treated as slaves. They were also the darkest-skinned. Just as America would do centuries later to Black people, India kept Dalits heavily segregated, with separate bathrooms and places to eat and drink.

This might seem a million miles away from the US police brutality against Black people that triggered the Black Lives Matter movement, but as Isabel Wilkerson points out in *Caste*, both share toxic origins. Wilkerson describes race as the 'unseen force of caste'. Where 'caste is the bones, race the skin'. Race is the visible signifier of the 'undesirable', while caste is the infrastructure that holds people of a certain race firmly in check, rooted in their place.

We know that caste and race have no real scientific basis. That they are social constructs. As James Baldwin, the American writer and activist, said, 'whiteness is just a metaphor for power'. Caste and race are often referred to as intractable systemic problems. This is true but also disingenuous, because who is the system? Who builds the structure? It's us. People. There is no faceless, nameless dystopian system grinding away, perpetuating discrimination while us humans stand helplessly by.

The reason that ending racism seems such a Herculean task is because it means dismantling these constructs and taking power away from the people who keep them going. These constructs are the foundations on which our political, social and economic systems have been built. Which means that removing them would cause many other things to collapse like a game of giant Jenga. You can bet your bottom dollar that the millions of people who would suddenly lose their advantage in the game of life are not going to let that happen easily.

Thus, race and caste are inextricably tied to social, political and economic inequality. In India, someone from a lower caste has no access to the inherited, generational wealth (both in financial terms, but also access to education and networks) that allows the higher castes to continue to thrive.

Think of it like this: being born into the lowest caste is like being in the sea in a rubber dinghy with holes. The only thing you are able to focus on is survival, by plugging those holes and staying afloat. Being in the highest caste is like being on a yacht. The waters may get choppy, but you'll always be above water. And you have the mental and physical space to think about anything that takes your fancy rather than pure survival.

From the very second a baby is born in India, his or her caste will determine the school they go to, whether or not they have the ability to go to university, whether those prestigious jobs they apply for are within reach or they are mysteriously turned down every time. It determines who they can marry. Where they can live. Even if they rise enough to go into politics, it dictates who will vote for them. The same is true, of course, for Black and brown people in the West, where their race can be a limiting factor.

People can 'escape' their caste, just as some people can overcome race-imposed disadvantages. But the battle is monumental. Kids of colour have been told for decades that they need to be twice as good as their peers. This pressure can be paralysing. If you feel you can never get *that* good, you're more likely to not want to try at all. Writing for *Vogue*, the Black American journalist Genelle Levy describes her fears of pursuing her dream to be a fashion editor because she thought 'I'm good but I'm not twice as good'. The stakes, as with the odds, are always higher for us.

I felt this pressure myself when I started my career as a science editor at *The Lancet*. This was the journalism equivalent of starting at the *New York Times* and I felt such an overwhelming pressure not to mess it up. Walking up the glass staircase of the *Lancet* offices in Camden, North London, I kept repeating the mantra, 'Do. Not. Fuck. This. Up.' Of course, everyone feels this way on the first day of a new job, but how many of you carry the added weight of feeling like you'll let your entire race down if you turn out to be unworthy?

As a woman of colour, I believed I had to work overtime to justify my place at the table. In the end, I probably succeeded far more than I ever would have done had I not had that pressure, but at the time, looking around at scientific conferences to see a sea of white faces, I had to constantly reassure myself that I belonged.

~

By moving to England, my parents removed me from many societal constraints I might have faced growing up in India, and I've had opportunities and freedoms I may never have had otherwise. And what England gave me was the ability to do exactly what I wanted with my life.

Between finishing my A levels at seventeen and starting university, I jumped on a plane to Spain where I worked as an au pair for six months. There was a practical reason for taking a year out of education. As we'd just moved back from India, in order to qualify for the free university education that the UK provided to its citizens (as extraordinary as that seems in today's world of mammoth student fees), I had to have been resident in England for three consecutive years. We had only been back for two years, so I was going to have to wait it out for a year.

This was not exactly a hardship. In between teaching English to Carmen and Manuel, my little Spanish charges, I drank cider in fields with Spanish teenagers, went to horse races with my host family and watched adrenaline-charged bullfights. A gap year like this would never have happened had I grown up in India. The societal pressures to throw myself immediately into studying to become one of the Holy Trinity (doctor, engineer or lawyer) would have been immense.

Exchanging letters with one of my best friends from India, Sonia, who was studying to be a doctor in Bangalore while I was still sunning myself in Spain listening to Tracy Chapman on repeat on my Walkman, she expressed her astonishment that I was 'wasting my life' with a gap year.

'You will lose an entire year!' she wrote. 'You're going to be so behind!!'

'Behind on what?' I wrote back, offended. 'We're young and life is long. By the time we're thirty, this won't make any difference to my career.' I'm pretty sure that was the last time we wrote to each other. Just two years before that, at sixteen, we had been the best of friends. We told each other everything. Had I remained in India, I might have thought like her too. In a country of 1.4 billion, where educational achievement is prized over almost anything else, the frenzied drive to push yourself and be the best could take on a manic edge.

Moving to England had opened my mind to bigger possibilities. Of living a life that didn't have to stick to a tightly drawn schedule.

For a brief moment after university, before I dived into an MSc in science communication, I had the urge to reject science altogether and become a reflexologist. I had done A levels in chemistry, biology and physics, but wasn't sure that being a laboratory researcher was really my next step – I was atrociously bad in the lab during my final-year project at university. My assignment had been to run genetic tests on embryonic mice samples to see whether they had possessed mutant genes. I would get so bored with the hours the tests took, I would sit in the common room with old copies of *Hello!* magazine. Frequently I would forget to stop the machine and the test would be a bust, which meant repeating it all over again. It didn't seem like a natural move to be in that environment all day, every day.

Reflexology was never really a serious consideration. Just me flailing around for something to do. My parents cautiously asked me if that was what I really wanted to pursue (I also carried tarot cards around and was permanently doused in patchouli, so I understand their hesitation). To their enormous credit, they didn't behave like most immigrant parents would when I supposed I might. They held back from offering up their opinion, and then let me come to my own realization that my destiny didn't perhaps have me sitting in a kaftan in a caravan, communicating with crystals.

I soon ran back to the familiar bosom of science, liberated by the idea that I was living in a time and place that meant I could do something that might actually change the world. I had already lived by myself in London – something my friends back in India could never have dreamt of doing as it wasn't 'seemly' for a young woman to live alone. I had gone to bars, got drunk, had my heart broken and gone on dodgy holidays to Greece with Vikki. The growing disparity between me and the alternate me who had remained in India was never far from my mind.

While I had a relatively strict upbringing, in the rearview mirror I can see how much freedom came with it. Even if that liberty always came with a frisson of guilt. If I kissed a boy on the first date, I imagined what my parents would think of me. When I got falling-down drunk from too many margaritas, I remembered Dad saying, 'You can drink whatever you want, but remember to never do anything you'd regret the next day.'

Sometimes, nothing shames children into behaving better than an understanding parent's quiet disappointment.

~

Living in England may have freed me from being constrained by caste, but having heritage from a country that is rife with discrimination is complicated and challenging and makes defining identity difficult.

As well as racism, Asian countries are also rampant with colourism, a word believed to have been coined in the 1980s by Pulitzer Prize-winning African-American writer Alice Walker. A cousin of caste and race, colourism is when lighter-skinned Black or brown people are treated more favourably than darker-skinned people.

Now that I live in Barcelona, and I get to see the Mediterranean sun most days, my skin colour is often the same as my sister, Poorna, who lives in England. When we lived in India, my skin had a much paler hue and my relatives often commented on it favourably even though it was just the amount of melanin in my skin I was born with.

'Such fair skin she has!' they would say, as if praising a prize cow. I hated it, given how many girls with darker skin would use dangerous bleaching creams on their face to blanch out the melanin to look more 'attractive'.

What I hated even more than praise for my pale skin was any commentary on Poorna's skin. Like Leela and

Shabby, Poorna's skin goes darker in the sun far more quickly than mine. I've long envied the ability to glow after just a few minutes in the sun, and would spend hours in the sun when I was younger in a bid to look the same. When Poorna faced comments like, 'Oh dear, you've really become burnt in the sun,' we'd both bristle, and hiss back, 'It's called a suntan. A sunburn is something totally different.'

In India, colourism plays out daily. Newspaper marriage adverts ask for prospective brides or grooms to have a 'wheatish complexion', which translates to 'please look as white as possible, thanks'. Mothers warn their children not to venture out into the sun for fear of 'becoming dark'. It took Shabby decades of cajoling to venture out of the shade on day trips, scarred by his mother apologizing to visiting relatives for him running around as a child in the sun getting dark. The abuse that dark-skinned South Asian people receive can be so extreme it damages their mental health and can make them self-harm or become suicidal.

The fact that colourism exists within brown and Black communities is akin to women being misogynists. Just as the patriarchy's peak achievement has been to make women internalize a misogyny that causes them to tear other women apart, colourism has been one of racism's greatest successes.

The oppressors don't even need to be present for people of colour to be subjugated, because after centuries of oppression, they are now experts at subjugating themselves.

13. Losing and Finding Myself, On Repeat

It's the end of a sticky summer day in Cinque Terre, Italy. Of the string of seaside villages that make up the *cinque* (five) *terre* (lands), we've chosen Monterosso for our family holiday. Every year, my parents, sister, Shabby, Leela and I go away for a few days together, and this holiday was shaping up to be one of our favourites so far.

After a day sunbathing on the orange-and-white-striped loungers, punctuated by many Aperol Spritzes and gelatos, we meander back to our hotel. We're all a bit frazzled by the sun and the several glasses of wine, but we don't want this night to end just yet. Our room has a private patio lit by fairy lights and we hang out here after dinner, opening more wine and putting some music on.

Mum and Dad love to dance, and are often the first on the dance floor. 'Come on, Leela, shake that booty!' my mum laughs, pulling Leela up to dance with her to Lizzo busting out 'Juice'.

I wish I could freeze this moment. To capture forever this time when the loves of my life are all around me, in a vortex of happiness.

Lizzo is Leela's current favourite singer, with her catchy lyrics and melodies, and the odd swear word that makes Leela giggle. But Leela loves her for another reason too. When I first played this track in the car, she became so obsessed she wanted to watch the music video when we got home.

She saw Lizzo dancing in a pink leotard and legwarmers and a light bulb went off in her head.

'Mama!' Leela squealed delightedly. 'She's brown just like me!'

'Yeah, she is,' I smiled. 'She's so beautiful, isn't she?'

Leela nodded, still enraptured by the video.

'Which other singers do we like who are brown?' she wondered.

'Well, there's my favourite, Beyoncé, and also Kelis, and before them I was obsessed with Whitney Houston and Neneh Cherry.'

I didn't point out that these global superstars were Black rather than of South Asian heritage as my little brown kid was seeing darker skin tones represented in some of the fiercest female musicians to ever exist and I didn't want to complicate that. Especially now that South Asian singers are starting to make it on to the global music scene, offering more representation for Leela.

This was the first time she'd seen that her skin colour could mean connection rather than isolation. I tried not to let my delight show too much in case it made her feel self-conscious. But as I cuddled Leela tight while she was watching the video, I let myself smile widely.

'Let's play Beyoncé,' she clapped.

~

We're now a couple of years on from that moment in the French supermarket, the day she first revealed unease in her own skin, and I'm thrilled that my campaign of representation is starting to pay off.

Before, it had felt a bit forced to try to buy a coffee-coloured Barbie, or books with brown kids in them, as it seemed like I was over-stressing the issue of race. Clearly, I was wrong. Ever since Elsa-braid-gate, I've made it my mission to show her positive representations of brown and Black people. I've surrounded her with children's books with protagonists of colour, bought her dolls that aren't just vanilla-coloured, taught her about Maya Angelou and the Indian maths prodigy Shakuntala Devi. About Mahatma Gandhi and Malcolm X. To show her that people who look like her have done great things and been incredible human beings.

When I studied science communication for my masters degree, one of the things we learnt about was semiotics, which is the study of how visual and linguistic signs create meaning. This gave me a behind-the-curtains look at marketing – every advert or film you see has subliminal messaging that embeds subconscious beliefs in us. In laundry detergent adverts, you'll see a lot of women holding up white clothes – symbolizing clean – and green or blue, if they are trying to denote science, for example because their soap is a new formulation. The advert might use imagery of men and mountains if they want you to believe their product is powerful and tough, i.e. masculine, in a patriarchal society's language. Archaic as that may sound, subliminal messaging is very much in use today, brainwashing kids with suggestible minds into seeing their place in the world. Racists regularly point out the UK has gone too far in terms of every advert showing mixed-race couples, Hollywood too far in having too many Black protagonists (they even dared to make a mermaid Black, the horror!), but our kids need this, and white children will grow up less intolerant seeing this normalized too.

If Leela could internalize the messaging from Disney about princesses mostly being white, I reasoned, she would absorb other ideas if I offered them up to her. And, over time, she has.

I don't doubt there will be bigger conversations about race and identity we'll need to have over the coming years, but finally she is comfortable in her own skin and celebrates it.

It occurs to me that she has an easier relationship with her identity than I do, and that maybe this isn't a bad thing.

My own sense of identity, especially when it comes to race, nationality and belonging, continually shifts and morphs. My relationship with England, the land of my birth, has been complex, and at times uneasy. It has been especially challenged in post-Brexit times to the point where my connection with the country has become frayed.

The duality of loving/not loving at the same time reflects how I feel about England. England has been a big part of my life, where I shared so many loves and laughter, shaping me to be the person I am today. I'd be lying to you and myself if I said I could turn my back on her forever.

Loving/not loving is a better description than calling it a love–hate relationship because there is never really hatred. It's more a disappointment, a disillusionment – a kind of falling out of love – with the increasingly intolerant country it is becoming. Or maybe it always was. Look at the former UK Home Secretary, Priti Patel. Easily one of the most racist politicians we've seen in power in our lifetime, yet one peek at the cesspit of social media and you can see they still call for her to be sent 'home'. When you look like us, regardless of whether you or even your parents were born here, there will always be those who will never truly consider us British.

'You're a citizen of the world,' Shabby tells Leela, when he's in a hippie frame of mind. 'You can be from wherever you want to be.'

Just as I had to figure out my own identity and my connection with my culture, so too will Leela. As she grows older, it will be up to her to negotiate her relationship with England, India and Bangladesh, France and Spain. And no matter how I think she should feel, or how I may want her to feel, what she chooses to hold on to and what she wants to discard is her decision alone.

What I can continue to teach her is the hard-won knowledge that has taken me a few decades to learn: the complexity of my identity is just who I am. I'm a product of my upbringing like anyone else, and if people can't immediately pin me down, if they can't instantly categorize me, well, that's okay.

I'm not a butterfly to be collected and labelled.

Feeling sometimes both British and Indian, and at other times feeling neither, is a state of mind I try to live with and even revel in, rather than fight. Not everyone belongs to two countries. What if I could look at it as having two cultures to cherry-pick from rather than being torn between them?

Society will always try to pin identities on us, but we can choose to reject them. And trying to make us choose between being one or the other is a false equivalence – we can be both. When I got divorced, I could have felt embarrassed and ashamed at vows made for life being broken less than five years later (and for a brief while I did), but in the end I refused to apologize for what was the right thing for both me and my ex-husband. I have many friends who were so emotionally destroyed by the tussle over money and property in their divorces, it left them unable to ever trust anyone again. I could have fought for a settlement; instead, I walked away from it all.

I was young and knew I could work hard, and so I chose to build a new life rather than haggle over my old one.

This will not define me, I promised myself, *I will rise like a goddamn phoenix from the ashes.*

When we lived in France and I worked for the UN with all that it brought in terms of status, salary, chunky pensions and my daughter's university fees paid for, I knew that a job which demanded so much of me, of my very bone marrow, until I had none left for my family, wasn't for me.

When I look back at my time on earth, my soul whispered to me, *I won't wish for my time in the office or more money. I will want more time with my Leela.*

Leaving France was not easy and shocked many of my colleagues, astonished that I would leave such security to become freelance. But in search of what me and my family really needed, we moved to Barcelona and I created a successful career in the middle of a pandemic.

This may sound boastful and like I'm offering up traditional markers of success – work, marriage, kids – as evidence of a good life. But it's actually the other way round. The things I have in my life now came to me when I rejected the norm and chose the life I really wanted.

When I walked away from a seemingly comfortable life, in search of a more authentic one.

I would never have got married again and had a child if I hadn't picked up the pieces of my life after my divorce and decided to live joyfully and with intent. I wouldn't be living in my dream city on the Mediterranean if I hadn't given up on money and security and bet on myself to be able to make a living by striking out as a freelancer.

~

Raising a child has been a journey in self-reflection and analysis. The answers to how to parent were never going to come from social media or parenting books, but from an honest interrogation of myself – what kind of child did I want to raise, and what kind of parent was

I willing to be in order to achieve that? This wasn't, and still isn't, easy.

It means reckoning with yourself and your baggage and your flaws frequently and honestly. It means constantly reassessing and recalibrating. It means letting go of the person you were before you became a parent.

It's not that motherhood changes you completely. But once another human being becomes your primary focus, your own internal circuitry is forever rewired to put them first, for your greatest hopes and fears to be about their life rather than yours. This doesn't make you weaker; the vulnerability that comes with having a child makes you stronger, more capable, more willing to fight.

And one day Leela will most likely have to fight her own battles against those who see her skin colour negatively. Traditionally there are two camps when it comes to this. An aggressive, radical, take-no-prisoners approach. And a touchy-feely, let's-talk-about-it-and-educate-people approach. Which is right? Probably both and neither at the same time. What the Black Lives Matter movement has shown is how white people still expect people of colour to do the work.

Where once many brown and Black people were made to do physical labour for free, now we are expected to do emotional and cultural labour for no reward. It's also shown me that peaceful demonstration and conversation will only get us so far. It's uncomfortable to admit, but when the structures we are trying to dismantle were built on blood, sweat and tears, literally standing on the bones of people of colour, how can we possibly think we won't need aggression to remove them?

By aggression, to make it clear, I'm not advocating looting and destruction or violence. I'm talking about a flat-out refusal to buy into existing structures that continue to try to keep us in our place. To push people of colour higher and higher, even if it comes at the expense of offending white people. I think this is one of the biggest battles we are fighting now: how uncomfortable are we willing to make white people?

How much are we willing to push those boundaries and barriers and say *No, you will not do this to me any more*?

~

One of the greatest joys of making new friends as an adult is when they convince you to try new things you would never have thought of. Sally, who is one of the most joyous women I know, has made me a convert to cold-water swimming. I have never before swum in the sea unless it's the temperature of a warm bath, but she tells me I will love being in the winter sea.

On New Year's Day 2022, we meet on the beach in Barcelona. It's a glorious 18°C and there are a few people around, parked on the sand or walking along the promenade.

No one is swimming.

But I'm in a bikini already, so I may as well. Sally, her boyfriend, Roger, and I all look at each other and then, in unison, run towards the still-chilly waters of the Mediterranean, which would not be warmed by the sun's rays for many months.

Seconds later, we are grinning like mad.

'Isn't this just the best?!' Sally shouts before she dives underwater.

'I absolutely love it!' I holler back.

People who love swimming in cold water talk about it like it's the best thing ever. Now I understand why: I have never felt more alive.

A few weeks later, I am back, this time with Leela. She has her swimsuit on, but looks dubious about swimming. We shake a towel out right by the edge of the sea and I bring out snacks and books and colouring pencils from the cavernous bag I seem to always carry as a mother.

I paddle in and try to coax her into the water.

'Are you sure you don't want to come in, Cookie? The water feels amazing. Once you're swimming, I promise you'll warm up.'

'Mmm, no thanks. I can sit here by myself. I'm a big girl,' she says proudly.

I swim for a few minutes, grateful, as I often am, to live where I do. It's a brand-new year and life feels rich with promise. I swim out a little way and look back to check that Leela is still okay.

She's lying on her tummy, her hair spooled out around her shoulders, drawing something and singing to herself.

Before I swim back to her, I talk to the sea, self-consciously at first, but then I realize the sound of the waves is drowning out my voice so no one else can hear me. I put words to my hopes and dreams, give them shape.

I've been trying to do this more lately and have even created a vision board. The idea of manifestation has drawn some derision from people who say that sitting on your arse and wishing for the moon is a fool's game. I see where they're coming from. Nothing manifests without effort, after all. The universe rarely reaches out to hand you your dreams on a plate.

But for me it's more about being brave enough to say what I want from life. And feeling like there's nothing wrong with me wanting to strive for more. Whether those goals are material, such as buying a little place in the countryside outside Barcelona, or emotional, like wanting to raise a kid who is happy and sure of herself.

Still feeling a little self-conscious, I put my hopes out there.

I just want Leela to feel safe and confident, I whisper to the sea.

I never want her to feel less than.

~

Leaving the water, I feel the watery sun try to warm my skin even as the winter breeze starts to chill me again. I get dressed hurriedly and lie down next to Leela.

'I love you, Leelee,' I tell her as I kiss her chocolate-brown cheeks. She has the softest skin, and I probably kiss it fifty times a day.

'I love you too, Mama,' she smiles back. 'Wait, who do you love the most, me or Daddy?' she asks mischievously, not for the first time. I insist, as always, that I love her and her father equally.

'I love me too.' Leela reflects on this. 'I actually love

myself the most. Then you and Daddy, Maiya and Otis, Aunty Poo, Ajja and Dodda . . .' She trails off.

I'm astonished that this kid has managed to grasp a concept that an entire billion-dollar self-help industry is based on. That self-love has to come before anything else. She's just seven, though. Surely she can't have come up with that herself? Maybe she heard it in a TV show? After all, children's programmes these days are more emotionally intelligent than the *Tom and Jerry* cartoons of my childhood.

'Who told you that you should love yourself first, Leela?'

She shrugs. 'My brain told me. I just know I love me,' she says, like it's the most obvious thing for her to believe. And then her mind darts off to less philosophical and more practical matters.

'Oooh, Mama, can we get an ice cream, please? Pleeeease?'

I don't know whether she heard someone talk about self-love, or overheard a conversation. However she got there, thank goodness she did.

For my kid to feel happy in her skin is all I've ever wanted. For her to love herself and know that's as important as loving anyone else? That's a bonus.

I know it doesn't end there, but there isn't a better place I could hope for her to start.

Acknowledgements

First, to my Mum and Dad. You have been such amazing parents to me that for a long time I thought everyone had parents like you – kind, supportive and funny, and always making me feel like I could do anything, could be anything. Then I grew up and realized just how special you both are, and that not everyone is as lucky as me. Every day, I try and raise Leela in the way you have shown me.

My dearest husband Shabby, this book would not have been written without you bringing me tea and breakfast every day in bed so I could write before work, without you taking on the lion's share of childcare and cooking dinner every night, and without your exceptional editorial eye in reading over drafts of this book. You believed in me even when I was on the verge of losing faith. I love you to the ends of the earth.

To the first children in my life, Maiya and Otis, my step-babies. You were my family even before I had Leela, and I love you.

To my sister Poorna, my womb-mate. This book wouldn't have been written without you either – when I nervously showed you a few paragraphs of an idea I had, your encouragement was what made me realize I had something worthwhile to say. Thank you for not letting me give up.

To my bestie Vikki, thank you for reading early chapters and giving me your honest feedback that helped me figure out how to tell this story.

Thank you to my amazing agent, Nelle Andrews, at Rachel Mills Literary and my wonderful publishers at Penguin Life, Martina and Susannah – you made the experience of writing a first book relatively painless.

Raising a baby truly takes a village. For the NCT mamas in my life – Sarah, Tor, Katy and Lisa – you literally and metaphorically held my hand in the early crazy days of motherhood. I would have been lost without you. My Ségny commune – Faith, Alice, Bernie and Jane – you were a critical support system for me in France when Leela was a tiny baby, and without you I would truly have lost my marbles.

And finally, to my heart, my little cookie dough, my darling Leela – you are my world. You are so funny, kind, sweet, clever and a million other things and I am so proud to be your mama. I love you to the moon and back.